PRAISE FOR *INTENTIONAL WALK*

"Most times, all fans get to see of the teams they root for is what happens on the field. But *Intentional Walk* goes behind the scenes and gives an intimate look on how members of the Cardinals organization deal with the ups and downs of everyday life. In my time with the Cardinals, I've seen numerous examples of guys leaning on their faith. I hope this book will give fans a little bit of insight into how these guys relate to each other and to God."

— John Mozeliak, general manager of the St. Louis Cardinals

"Baseball players are typically defined by what they do on the mound, in the field, or at the plate. However, this doesn't always accurately define who these men really are. *Intentional Walk* does a wonderful job of painting a picture of members of the Cardinals organization and what they want to define them. As fans enjoy this book, I hope they take notice of the priority these men place on their relationship with Jesus Christ."

— Andy Benes, fourteen-year Major League Baseball pitcher and former St. Louis Cardinal

"Rob Rains captures the joy of being a follower of Christ in a fantastic way as he chronicles the faith of over a dozen Cardinals in *Intentional Walk*. Each person featured has a unique story to tell of his relationship with Jesus and how he lives out his walk with Him on and off the field.

"Writing this book was a labor of love for Rob. His desire to share the stories of this group of men is an encouragement not only to St. Louis Cardinal fans but to everyone who enjoys reading about God's amazing power to change lives in profound ways."

— Vince Nauss, president of Baseball Chapel

"Discipline, humility, good coaching, support during the tough times, faith . . . These aren't just the building blocks for assembling championship baseball teams; they are the cornerstones for constructing a meaningful life.

"Both goals start with a faith in God, as author Rob Rains demonstrates in *Intentional Walk*, an honest, perhaps controversial look at one of the driving forces behind the 2012 St. Louis Cardinals' effort to capture a second consecutive World Series championship. In a high-pressure sport where the best fail seven of ten times at the plate, *Intentional Walk* demonstrates how faith in God and His teachings provided the sort of balance and peace in the Cardinals' lives that allowed them to perform at their best—win or lose. The personal, heartfelt stories Rains shares in *Intentional Walk* are a lesson for all of us, no matter our profession."

— Curtis Eichelberger, author of *Men of Sunday: How Faith Guides the Players, Coaches & Wives of the NFL*

INTENTIONAL WALK

INTENTIONAL

WALK

An Inside Look at the
Faith That Drives the
St. Louis Cardinals

ROB RAINS

THOMAS NELSON
Since 1798

NASHVILLE   DALLAS   MEXICO CITY   RIO DE JANEIRO

Published in Nashville, Tennessee, by Thomas Nelson. Thomas Nelson is a registered trademark of Thomas Nelson, Inc.

Thomas Nelson, Inc., titles may be purchased in bulk for educational, business, fundraising, or sales promotional use. For information, please e-mail SpecialMarkets@ ThomasNelson.com.

Any Internet addresses, phone numbers, or company or product information printed in this book are offered as a resource and are not intended in any way to be or to imply an endorsement by Thomas Nelson, nor does Thomas Nelson vouch for the existence, content, or services of these sites, phone numbers, companies, or products beyond the life of this book.

Scripture quotations marked ESV are from The Holy Bible, English Standard Version® (ESV®), copyright © 2001 by Crossway, a publishing ministry of Good News Publishers. Used by permission. All rights reserved.

Scripture quotations marked KJV are from the King James Version of the Bible.

Scripture quotations marked NASB are from the NEW AMERICAN STANDARD BIBLE®, © The Lockman Foundation 1960, 1962, 1963, 1968, 1971, 1972, 1973, 1975, 1977, 1995. Used by permission.

Scripture quotations marked NCV are from the New Century Version®. © 2005 by Thomas Nelson, Inc. Used by permission. All rights reserved.

Scripture quotations marked NIV are taken from the Holy Bible, New International Version®, NIV®. Copyright © 1973, 1978, 1984, 2011 by Biblica, Inc.™ Used by permission of Zondervan. All rights reserved worldwide. www.zondervan.com

Scripture quotations marked NKJV are from THE NEW KING JAMES VERSION. © 1982 by Thomas Nelson, Inc. Used by permission. All rights reserved.

Scripture quotations marked WEB are taken from the World English Bible.

ISBN: 978-0-8499-6458-9

Library of Congress Control Number: 2012955284

Printed in the United States of America

13 14 15 16 17 RRD 6 5 4 3 2 1

CONTENTS

PROLOGUE

On the morning of March 5, 2012, the white Chevrolet Suburban pulled into the reserved spot in the parking lot at Roger Dean Stadium in Jupiter, Florida, shortly after 4:00 a.m.

Mike Matheny had not really planned to get to the ballpark that early, but when he had awoken an hour earlier, he knew it would be futile to try to go back to sleep.

Matheny's excitement was genuine. Even though he had already spent a couple of weeks as the Cardinals' new manager, in charge of the daily workouts at the team's spring training complex, this day was different. There was a game to play—against the Miami Marlins—and even though the result of the team's first exhibition game of the spring would be basically meaningless for almost everybody involved, Matheny knew it would be a day he would never forget.

Ever since getting the phone call from general manager John Mozeliak in November 2011, while he was in a barrio in the Dominican Republic, Matheny had thought about this day and had been preparing for it. Mozeliak had called to offer Matheny the job of managing the St. Louis Cardinals, succeeding future Hall of Famer Tony La Russa. It was an offer Matheny quickly accepted.

The offer was not without risk—the Cardinals were the defending world champions, and Mozeliak knew he was taking a chance giving the job to a man who, at forty-one, not only would become the youngest manager in the major leagues, but had never coached or managed a single day at any level above Little League. What mattered more to Mozeliak, and to the team's primary owner and chairman, Bill DeWitt, however, was the character of the man they were hiring. Those intangible skills, both believed, far outweighed the lack of managerial experience. In Matheny, both Mozeliak and DeWitt knew they were hiring a man of principle, a man born and trained to be a leader, a man of God who valued the importance of relationships.

"This is not meant for everyone," Mozeliak said at the news conference announcing Matheny's appointment. "For a lot of people, this might be a very difficult task to tackle. With any decision you make at this level, there are risks. And there are in this as well. But I do think he is very capable of succeeding in this role."

Added DeWitt, who first got to know Matheny as a player with the Cardinals, "All great managers started somewhere. I think the lack of experience is there. Any time you do something new, it's an unknown. What we were looking for are characteristics that would make a manager successful. And he's got those."

At the time Matheny was hired, nobody knew that his close friend, former teammate and three-time National League MVP Albert Pujols, would decide to sign with the Los Angeles Angels as a free agent. Nobody knew that the team's longtime pitching coach, Dave Duncan, would decide to leave the team to care for his wife as she battled brain cancer instead of standing beside the rookie manager in the team's dugout. As Matheny prepared for spring training, however, he made the decision not to dwell on who was not going to be in the Cardinals' camp, but instead to concentrate on who *was* there.

It was an attitude and a philosophy he quickly passed on to his players, and one they bought into without hesitation. So instead of writing Pujols's name on the lineup card for that first spring game, Matheny had twenty-three-year-old rookie Matt Adams playing first and batting sixth. The new manager was eager to see a player he had watched tear up Double-A the previous season step onto the major league stage.

As he sat in the quiet of his office that March morning, Matheny did what he had been doing daily since arriving in Jupiter. He used the early-morning hours for personal reflection and to read the Bible.

His occupation might have changed over the winter, but Matheny had not changed. His faith and his family had always been the two most important aspects of Matheny's life, and he was not going to let his new position change that.

He was the same man who, as a twenty-one-year-old Class A player in 1992 in Stockton, California, was one of several players who went to team owner Dick Phelps and negotiated a five-dollar raise in daily meal money for the team. Years later, Phelps recalled that Matheny was the only player who came by to thank him.

"At that age, Mike already had the rest of the players' respect," Phelps said.

He was the same man who, years later, was playing golf at an exclusive country club near St. Louis when one of his shots went way out of bounds and tore a hole in the screen porch of a house overlooking the course. Instead of just dropping a new ball and continuing on, Matheny did something only a select few people would do.

"Mike drove the cart up to the house and left a note with his name and phone number and told the owner to contact him and he would pay for the damages," said Cardinals broadcaster Rick Horton, who was playing with Matheny on that day. "The lady ended up calling him, and he took care of it. That's just the kind of person Mike is."

When Mozeliak had called to offer the Cardinals managing job to him, Matheny was on a goodwill trip to the Dominican Republic with his fourteen-year-old son, Jacob. Two of his other sons, Luke and Blaise, were also on the trip. It was almost fitting that Matheny got the job while coaching a youth team, since that had been his only managerial experience. What Mozeliak, DeWitt, and all of Matheny's friends and former teammates already knew, however, was that the way Matheny ran those Little League teams was, in many ways, similar to how he would run a major league team. The ability of the players might be different, and the stakes a little higher, but the way Matheny went about his business and his approach to life and baseball would not change.

That was evident from a letter Matheny wrote to the parents of the other youths on the first Little League team he managed, a couple of years after his playing career ended in 2006. The letter read:

> *I always said that the only team that I would coach would be a team of orphans, and now here we are. The reason for me saying this is that I have found the biggest problem with youth sports has been the parents. I think that it is best to nip this in the bud right off the bat. I think the concept that I am asking all of you to grab is that this experience is ALL about the boys. If there is anything about it that includes you, we need to make a change of plans. My main goals are as follows:*
>
> *(1) to teach these young men how to play the game of baseball the right way,*
> *(2) to be a positive impact on them as young men, and*
> *(3) do all of this with class.*

We may not win every game, but we will be the classiest coaches, players, and parents in every game we play. The boys are going to play with a respect for their teammates, opposition, and the umpires, no matter what.

With that being said, I need to let you know where I stand. I have no hidden agenda. I have no ulterior motive other than what I said about my goals. I also need all of you to know that my priorities in life will most likely be a part of how I coach, and the expectations I have for the boys. My Christian faith is the guide for my life and I have never been one for forcing my faith down someone's throat, but I also believe it to be cowardly, and hypocritical, to shy away from what I believe. You as parents need to know for yourselves, and for your boys, that when the opportunity presents itself, I will be honest with what I believe. That may make some people uncomfortable, but I did that as a player, and I hope to continue it in any endeavor that I get into. I am just trying to get as many potential issues out in the open from the beginning. I believe that the biggest role of the parent is to be a silent source of encouragement. I think if you ask most boys what they would want their parents to do during the game, they would say, "Nothing."

Once again, this is ALL about the boys. I believe that Little League parents feel that they must participate with loud cheering and "Come on, let's go, you can do it," which just adds more pressure to the kids. I will be putting plenty of pressure on these boys to play the game the right way with class, and respect, and they will put too much pressure on themselves and each other already. You as parents need to be the silent, constant source of support.

Let the record state right now that we will not have good umpiring. This is a fact, and the sooner we all understand that, the better off we will be. We will have balls that bounce in the dirt that will be called strikes, and we will have balls over our heads that will be called strikes. Likewise, the opposite will happen with the strike zone while we are pitching. The boys will not be allowed, at any time, to show any emotion against the umpire. They will not shake their head, or pout, or say anything to the umpire. This is my job, and I will do it well. I once got paid to handle those guys, and I will let them know when they need to hear something. I am really doing all of you parents a favor that you probably don't realize at this point. I have taken out any work at all for you except to get them there on time, and enjoy. The thing that these boys need to hear is that you enjoyed watching them and you hope that they had fun. I know that it is going to be very hard not to coach from the stands and yell encouraging things to your son, but I am confident that this works in a negative way for their development and their enjoyment. Trust me on this. I am not saying that you cannot clap for your kids when they do well. I am saying that if you hand your child over to me to coach them, then let me do that job.

A large part of how your child improves is your responsibility. The difference for kids at this level is the amount of repetition that they get. This goes with pitching, hitting, and fielding. As a parent, you can help out tremendously by playing catch, throwing batting practice, hitting ground balls, or finding an instructor who will do this in your place. The more of this your kids can get, the better. This is the one constant that I have found with players that reached the major leagues . . . someone spent time with them away from the field.

I am completely fine with your son getting lessons from whomever you see fit. The only problem I will have is if your instructor is telling your son not to follow the plan of the team. I will not teach a great deal of mechanics at the beginning, but I will teach mental approach, and expect the boys to comply. If I see something that your son is doing mechanically that is drastically wrong, I will talk with the instructor and clear things up. The same will hold true with pitching coaches. We will have a pitching philosophy and will teach the pitchers and catchers how to call a game, and why we choose the pitches we choose. There is no guessing. We will have a reason for the pitches that we throw. A pitching coach will be helpful for the boys to get their arms in shape and be ready to throw when spring arrives. Every boy on this team will be worked as a pitcher. We will not overuse these young arms and will keep close watch on the number of innings that the boys are throwing.

I will be throwing so much info at these boys that they are going to suffer from overload for a while, but eventually they are going to get it. I am a stickler about the thought process of the game. I will be talking nonstop about situational hitting, situational pitching, and defensive preparation. The question that they are going to hear the most is, "What were you thinking?" What were you thinking when you threw that pitch? What were you thinking during that at-bat? What were you thinking before the pitch was thrown? Were you anticipating anything?

I am a firm believer that this game is more mental than physical, and the mental may be more difficult, but can be taught and can be learned by ten- and eleven-year-olds. If it sounds like I am going to be demanding of these boys, you are exactly right. I am definitely demanding their attention, and the other thing that I am going to require is effort. Their attitudes, their concentration, and their effort are the things that they can control. If they give me these things every time they show up, they will have a great experience.

The best situation for all of us is for you to plan on handing these kids over to me and the assistant coaches when you drop them off, and plan on them being mine for the two or so hours that we have scheduled for a game, or the time that we have scheduled for the practice. I would like for these boys to have some responsibility for having their own water, not needing you to keep running to the concession stand, or having parents behind the dugout asking their sons if they are thirsty, or hungry, or too hot, and I would appreciate if you would share this information with other invited guests, such as grandparents. If there is an injury, obviously we will get you to help, but besides that, let's pretend that they are at work for a short amount of time and that you have been granted the pleasure of watching. I will have them at games early so we can get stretched and loosened up, and I will have a meeting with just the boys after the game. After the meeting, they are all yours again. As I am writing this, I realize I sound like the Little League Nazi, but I believe that this will make things easier for everyone involved.

I truly believe that the family is the most important institution in the lives of these guys. With that being said, I think that the family events are much more important than the sports events. I just ask that you are considerate of the rest of the team and let the team manager and myself know when you will miss, and to let us know as soon as possible. I know that there will be times when I am going to miss either for family reasons or for other commitments. If your son misses a game or a practice, it is not the end of the world, but there may be some sort of repercussion, just out of respect for the kids that put the effort into making it. The kind of repercussions could possibly be running, altered playing time, or position in the batting order.

Speaking of batting order, I would like to address that right from the top as well, seeing that next to playing time this is the second most complained-about issue, or actually tied for second with position on the defensive field. Once again, I need you to know that I am trying to develop each boy individually, and I will give him a chance to learn and play any position that he is interested in. I also believe that this team will be competitive, and when we get into situations where we are focusing on winning, like a tournament for example, we are going to put the boys in the position that will give the team the best opportunity. I will talk with the boys individually and have them tell me what their favorite positions are and what other positions they would like to learn about. As this season progresses, there is a chance that your son may be playing a position that he doesn't necessarily like, but I will need your support about his role on the team. I know that times have changed, but one of the greatest lessons that my father taught me was that my coach was always right . . . even when he was wrong. This principle is a great life lesson about how things really work. I hope that I will have enough humility to come to your son if I treated him wrong and apologize. Our culture has lost this respect for authority, mostly because the kids hear the parents constantly complaining about the teachers and coaches of the child.

I need all of you to know that we are most likely going to lose many games this year. The main reason is that we need to find out how we measure up with the local talent pool. The only way to do this is to play against some of the best teams. I am convinced that if the boys put their work in at home, and give me their best effort, that we will be able to play with just about any team. Time will tell. l also believe that there is enough local talent that we will not have to do a large amount of travel, if any. This may be disappointing for those of you who only play baseball and look forward to the out-of-town experiences, but I also know that this is a relief for the parents that have traveled throughout the United States and Canada for hockey and soccer, looking for better competition. In my experiences, we have traveled all over the Midwest and have found just as good competition right in our backyard. If this season goes well, we will entertain the idea of travel in the future.

The boys will be required to show up ready to play every time they come to the field. Shirts tucked in, hats on straight, and pants not drooping down to their knees. There is not an excuse for lack of hustle on a baseball field. From the first step outside the dugout they will hustle. They will have a fast jog to their positions, to the plate, and back to the bench when they make an out. We will run out every hit harder than any team we will play, and will learn how to always back up a play to help our teammates. Every single play, every player will be required to move to a spot. Players that do not hustle and run out balls will not play. The boys will catch on to this quickly. The game of baseball becomes very boring when players are not thinking about the next play and what they possibly could do to help the team. Players on the bench will not be messing around. I will constantly be talking with them about situations and what they would be doing if they were in a specific position, or if they were the batter. There is as much to learn on the bench as there is on the field if the boys want to learn. All of this will take some time for the boys to conform to. They are boys, and I am not trying to take away from that, but I do believe that they can bear down and concentrate hard for just a little while during the games and practices.

I know this works because this was how I was taught the game, and how our parents acted in the stands. We started our Little League team when I was ten years old in a little suburb of Columbus, Ohio. We had a very disciplined coach that expected the same from us. We committed eight summers to this man and we were rewarded for our efforts. I went to Michigan, another player went to Duke, one to Miami of Florida, two went to North Carolina, one went to Central Florida, one went to Kent State, and most of the others played smaller Division I or II baseball. Four of us went on to play professionally. This was coming from a town where no one had ever been recruited by any colleges. I am not saying that this is what is going to happen to our boys, but what I do want you to see is that this system works. I know that right now you are asking yourself if this is what you want to get yourself into, and I understand that for some of you it may not be the right fit. I also think that there is a great opportunity for these boys to grow together and learn some lessons that will go beyond

their baseball experience. Let me know as soon as possible whether
or not this is a commitment that you and your son want to make.

Thanks,
Mike

Matheny was speaking from his heart in the letter. He wanted to have an open relationship with the players on his team and their parents, and he knew he could not be anything other than himself. That was how he had always been, dating back to when he was growing up as a Little Leaguer himself in Reynoldsburg, Ohio, a suburb of Columbus.

"The story really starts with two very humble parents who were smart enough to realize the truth," Matheny said. "God opened their eyes to the kind of life they needed to lead. They were very consistent with how they went about that on a daily basis with two young eyes constantly watching them."

Matheny's father, Jerry, was a construction worker who grew up on a farm in the hills of West Virginia, taught to love baseball by his father. Jerry was a good enough baseball player, his son says, to get tryouts with several teams, including the Pittsburgh Pirates, but when nothing came of it, he joined a construction crew, got married, and started raising a family. He passed along his passion for baseball to Mike and his three brothers.

It was from his parents that Matheny learned the value of working hard, and the importance of putting in an honest day of work, in addition to his religious foundation. It was at a church service when he was about nine years old that Matheny made the advanced decision that he wanted to have God in control of his life, that he wanted to have a relationship with Him.

"We had a guest speaker that Sunday, a man from the South," Matheny said. "He was waving his Bible around and pounding on the podium, and kept saying over and over again, 'Who is Jesus to you?' I kept thinking, *This guy is in the wrong place. We know who Jesus is. We are always here, we know all the songs, we know when to sit down and stand up.*

"He kept saying, 'Who is Jesus to you? I don't care who your parents are or what your pedigree is—who is He to you? Do you know Him?'"

After the church service was over and Matheny had returned home, the questions kept coming back to him. It had seemed to him that the preacher was looking and speaking directly at him.

"I finally got up enough courage to go out and ask my parents about it," Matheny said. "I asked them some pretty deep questions, and they got out the Bible and gave me the truth. They opened up the book of Romans and led me through the gospel. I made a decision right then and there that 'I want this. I want Him, not just in my head, not just knowing who He is, but I want Him in my life.'"

The relationship Matheny started that day with God has been with him ever since, through good times and bad, helping him cope with whatever hand he was dealt in life.

God was there when Matheny made the decision to turn down a contract offer from the Toronto Blue Jays after high school, instead opting to accept a scholarship to the University of Michigan. It was a decision Matheny prayed long and hard about, even as he drove from his home to Ann Arbor for the start of fall classes, and as he unpacked in his new dormitory room. As he prepared to leave the room for his first class, Matheny knew he was making a decision that could affect him the rest of his life. There was no guarantee he would get another shot at playing professional baseball, his dream since he had been a young boy watching games on television. He knew he was making a commitment to spend at least the next three years at Michigan before he would even have the chance to be drafted again.

"It crossed my mind that I might never get a shot again," he said, "but education meant a lot to me—and still does."

Matheny picked up the telephone in his room and called Pat Gillick, the Toronto general manager, to tell him he had made his final decision to go to school. As he grabbed his backpack and headed out the door to attend his first class, Matheny said another quick prayer that God would send him a sign that he had made the right choice.

Almost as soon as he got out the door, a large pigeon pooped directly on his head. Others walking by saw what had happened and started laughing.

"I'm not talking a little bit, I'm talking Nickelodeon stuff," Matheny recalled years later in an interview with the Michigan student newspaper. "I was completely covered. I was thinking, *God, I asked You to be clear before, but c'mon.*"

Matheny had to go back to his room and change clothes, which gave him one more chance to change his mind and call Toronto and accept the offer of a $100,000 signing bonus. He did not pick up the phone, and again headed out for his first college class, arriving about twenty minutes late.

Matheny soon realized the sign he had asked God about came in the form of a young blonde woman sitting in that class. He quickly started a conversation with Kristin, a field hockey player from St. Louis. Matheny didn't know it at the time, but a few years later Kristin would become his wife and the mother of his children.

During Matheny's sophomore year, former All-Star catcher Bill Freehan, who had spent fifteen years in the major leagues, became the Michigan coach. He quickly identified Matheny as one of the team leaders and a man he thought had a future in the game. One day he called Matheny in for a meeting in his office. Freehan's instructions were simple. He told Matheny to schedule a meeting with his guidance counselor, and from then on to make certain all his elective courses were Spanish classes. Freehan knew that having the ability to speak Spanish would give Matheny a major advantage if he pursued a baseball career, and he was right.

Matheny went on to earn his degree in sports management from Michigan, with an emphasis in Spanish—a skill he uses on a daily basis.

Matheny played well enough during his three years with the Wolverines that he did get that second chance at a baseball career. The Milwaukee Brewers drafted him in the eighth round in 1991, and within three years he was playing in the major leagues.

One new teammate who began to notice Matheny immediately was Kevin Seitzer, who, twenty-one years later, in 2012, was serving as the Royals' hitting coach. One day in that first spring training everybody on the team noticed Matheny.

"He was catching, and a hitter tried to charge the mound," Seitzer recalled. "The hitter never got past the plate. Mike took him down. He was on him so quick the guy never had a chance. That was something that impressed all of us, especially our manager, Phil Garner. We had a catcher get hurt at the end of the spring, and Mike ended up making the club."

Because Seitzer's family would not join him in Milwaukee until the school year was out, he invited Matheny to move into his two-bedroom apartment.

"I had already seen what kind of kid he was," Seitzer said. "I knew he was a Christian, and I was a Christian. I took care of him as long as he was there. We had a special bond; he was kind of like my little brother. I wouldn't let him pay for anything, and it drove him crazy."

The two talked daily about baseball, and almost as often about God and religion. Seitzer shared his testimony with Matheny, about how he didn't find or develop a relationship with God until he had already been in the majors for several years.

"I reached the pot of gold at the end of the rainbow and realized there was something missing," Seitzer said. "I was crazy—a partying, cussing, just intense, off-the-charts crazy. I had grown up in church, but never knew anything about having a relationship with Him. Mike was already there. Even then he was very bold and never made any ifs, ands, or buts about where he stands with his faith."

Matheny went on to play in the majors for thirteen years with the Brewers, the Toronto Blue Jays, the St. Louis Cardinals, and the San Francisco Giants before a series of concussions finally forced him to retire in 2006 at the age of thirty-four. The effects of the concussions lingered for several months, and often Matheny would forget simple things, like what he was supposed to get at the grocery store or where he had left his car keys. One time he was in his car and forgot how to get home. But through all of those trials and tribulations, Matheny's faith never wavered that one day he would recover.

Matheny's faith had never been stronger than when he decided to manage the Cardinals. He knew on that day that his faith would be tested in more ways than he could ever imagine, and he prayed that God would give him the understanding and guidance he knew he would need to be successful in his new job. He also made certain that every one of his players knew exactly what they were getting in their new manager.

"During one of our first meetings in the spring, I sat the guys down and made it very clear," Matheny said. "I made a promise to them. I am who I am. I am not going to shove my faith down your throat, but when the opportunity presents itself, don't expect me to walk away. This is who I am, and Jesus Christ is at the center of my life. It's all that I am, every day, every decision that I make. I'm going to stand up and tell you what I believe is true."

As he had done as a player, and as he had done as a son,

husband, and father, Matheny pledged to himself and to God that he would do everything in his power to become a good manager. He didn't just want to do a good job; he wanted to do a great job because he knew that was what God expected from him.

"I think it is our responsibility to go out and do everything we can, every minute, to excel in whatever arena we are put in," Matheny said. "I think we should all be very attentive to what is going on around us and the opportunities that are there.

"I believe, in every aspect of my life, that I am called to excellence. I believe through my faith that I am called to high expectations as a husband and as a father. This job is a test to my faith every day, but I believe if I stay consistent with everything I do in my life, I will be the best manager I can be if I am true to who I say I am. I want to just be consistent with how I serve these guys and be consistent with the effort I put in. I have accountability not only to these guys, but to myself."

Matheny knew he was fortunate to be taking over a team with a roster filled with strong Christians. During spring training, as many as ten Cardinals gathered two or three times a week at 5:30 a.m. to share their faith with one another. Wednesday night was family Bible study night, open to minor leaguers as well, and the meeting room was always packed.

As the spring came to an end and the dawn of the regular season arrived, Matheny and his players were ready to see what would happen in the 2012 season.

ONE

DAVID FREESE

The Lord is my shepherd; I shall not want.

He maketh me to lie down in green pastures: he leadeth me beside the still waters.

He restoreth my soul: he leadeth me in the paths of righteousness for his name's sake.

Yea, though I walk through the valley of the shadow of death, I will fear no evil: for thou art with me; thy rod and thy staff they comfort me.

Thou preparest a table before me in the presence of mine enemies: thou anointest my head with oil; my cup runneth over.

Surely goodness and mercy shall follow me all the days of my life: and I will dwell in the house of the Lord for ever.

—Psalm 23 KJV

The night before the Cardinals played their opening game of the 2012 regular season on April 4, the first-ever game at Marlins Park in Miami, a visiting reporter walked into a well-known restaurant to have dinner. It was not surprising to him that some of the Cardinals were there. What he was astounded by, however, was that a dozen of the players were there having dinner, together, at the same table.

Despite having covered baseball for about thirty years, this was not something the reporter was used to seeing, and it spoke volumes to him about the 2012 Cardinals, the closeness of the players, and the chemistry and the bond that connected this team.

David Freese was one of the players there that night, along with many of the team's veterans, including Matt Holliday, Adam Wainwright, and Chris Carpenter.

"A lot of the veterans get together and they drag me along," Freese has said. "It's a free meal."

Freese, of course, may never have to buy a meal in St. Louis again after his heroics in the 2011 postseason, which included hitting the walk-off home run in the eleventh inning of game six, perhaps one of the most dramatic moments in World Series history.

There was more involved on that April night, however, than the fact that Freese didn't have to pay for his steak and lobster—the team's players try to get together for dinner at least once on every road trip during the season, and as many players who want to come are welcome.

"It's a great time for fellowship," Freese said. "The coolest thing about this group is our fellowship together. That's a big word in our clubhouse. What I hear is that it is very unusual in baseball, but what we have here with our spiritual faith is a good thing. It keeps you grounded. It keeps you on the right path.

"You definitely can identify with what's important in the world when you step in this clubhouse."

This is particularly important for Freese, who is aware of a couple of points in his life, both in baseball and outside the game, when he could have gone in a much different direction, had he allowed himself to continue down a bad path.

Continuing down the wrong road definitely would have led Freese to a different place than Busch Stadium, in his hometown of St. Louis, where his performance during one magical October made him a hometown hero as well as an overnight national and international celebrity.

Appearances on *The Tonight Show with Jay Leno* and other television shows followed his selection as the MVP of both the National League Championship Series against the Milwaukee Brewers and the World Series against the Texas Rangers. Anybody and everybody wanted a piece of Freese, who claims one of his most chilling moments came in November 2011, when he was on the field for the Missouri–Texas football game and received a prolonged standing ovation from more than seventy thousand fans.

Freese knew then, and knows now, that none of it would have been possible had he not made a dramatic decision in December 2009 to turn his life over to Christ. He had just been involved in a second off-field incident, which was embarrassing to himself, his family, and the Cardinals. After a heartfelt talk with his parents, he made an unannounced trip to the stadium to talk with general manager John Mozeliak, offering a sincere apology and a pledge that it would not happen again.

Then the twenty-six-year-old Freese went home and walked into his bedroom. He was drained and exhausted. "I didn't have much left," Freese said.

He sat down and prayed.

"I really kind of surrendered myself," Freese recalled. "I said, 'God, here I am. Do with me what You will. I'm Yours.' I look back at that now and realize that was a very big moment in my life."

At the time, Freese had only played seventeen games in the major leagues with the Cardinals. He had not been a high bonus baby, having been drafted in the ninth round by the San Diego Padres out of South Alabama in June 2006. The Cardinals had obtained him the previous winter, in Mozeliak's first trade as general manager, for outfielder Jim Edmonds.

The Cardinals believed Freese had a chance to become a

regular third baseman in the majors, but only if he could straighten up his personal life and also avoid frequent injuries. It was shortly after making the decision to turn his life over to Christ that Freese just "happened" to run into Matheny at a charity bowling event in St. Louis, organized by former major leaguer Brian Boehringer.

"It was a great time to run into Mike Matheny," Freese said. Matheny at the time was living in St. Louis and working as a special instructor in the Cardinals' farm system. Freese had been a fan of Matheny's a decade earlier, often watching from the upper deck as Matheny played for the Cardinals.

"He pulled me aside and talked to me for about twenty minutes," Freese said. "That was when our relationship really catapulted. We went on from there, and it has been good things ever since."

Freese knows now that the meeting was not accidental. After his meeting and conversation with Matheny, Freese began to notice a gradual change in his life.

"There were people who started entering my life after that," Freese said, "and that's when I really started to notice that God had a plan . . . that He's got an idea for you. I can sit down right now and tell you that ten years ago I probably had five hundred more friends, but the friends I have now mean more to me. The relationships run deeper."

Freese knows that because of the people God put into his life, his life has been changed.

"I don't know what would have happened [without Christ in my life]," Freese said. "This world is crazy. You don't know what can happen. I can tell you right now I wouldn't be in this position, personally or professionally.

"Sometimes I get caught up in saying, why didn't I find God earlier in my life, and I know that's just not God's plan sometimes. That's frustrating for me to think about, but what I have gone through has put me in this position, not just professionally but personally. The relationships I've built, the sense of joy I have internally compared to ten years ago—that's appealing to me."

That December 2009 incident—the wake-up call—that jolted Freese was not the first time he had wondered about his baseball future.

Years earlier, after his senior year at Lafayette High School in suburban St. Louis, after earning All-State honors and receiving multiple scholarship offers, Freese decided baseball was no longer fun. He wanted to go to the University of Missouri, but he wanted to, in his words, "be a regular kid" and not have his college life dictated by the team's schedule.

For the first time in his life, Freese did not play baseball that year. He joined a fraternity, and enjoyed his break from the daily grind of practice, training, and games. He did not think about it at the time, but Freese knows and understands now that making that decision, one he said only his parents supported, was also a part of God's plan for his life.

"If I had kept playing, it would have been because I was listening to everybody else," he said. "At that time, it was nice to be selfish and stubborn. You don't want to be those things, but at that time it was what I needed to be, especially when I can look back and see where I am now."

Sometime before the next school year began, Freese had a change of heart. He doesn't remember it being because of one specific incident, but he came to the conclusion that he missed playing baseball. The year away had forced him to reassess a lot of priorities in his life. Instead of returning to Missouri, he enrolled at a local junior college in the St. Louis area, Meramec Community College, and started working harder than he had ever worked at the game before. If he was going to play baseball, he wanted to succeed at the highest level.

Freese knows now that the inspiration behind that decision was God-driven. "It was just something I felt like I needed to do," he said. "I needed to play baseball. I needed to find out what I was all about. Honestly, when I started back playing, I was not entirely sure that was what I wanted to do. It took the two years at Meramec to realize that I love this game."

Two good years at the junior-college level led to the scholarship offer from South Alabama, where Freese hit .414 and soon found himself signing a contract to play in the Padres organization.

He spent the 2006 and 2007 seasons playing in Eugene, Oregon; Fort Wayne, Indiana; and Lake Elsinore, California, and was pleased with how his career was progressing. That December he was having dinner with friends at a Burger King in suburban Los Angeles when his cell phone rang.

Freese saw that the call was coming from the St. Louis area, but he didn't recognize the number, so he let it go to voice mail. When he checked the message moments later, the caller identified himself as John Mozeliak, the general manager of the Cardinals, who said he was calling to welcome Freese to the organization.

Freese thought it was one of his friends pulling a prank on him. But before he could figure out who it could be, his phone rang again. He took the call, from the San Diego area, and quickly learned that the first call had not been a prank. He really had been traded to the Cardinals.

After that reality set in, Freese called home to tell his mother the news. She, like her son, thought it was a joke until he convinced her otherwise.

"I can't tell you everything she said, but she definitely didn't believe it," Freese said.

Freese made the jump from the Class A California League to Triple-A Memphis in 2008 and had a big year, hitting .306 with 26 homers and 91 RBI. It looked as if the Cardinals had found their third baseman of the future, perhaps beginning as soon as 2009. That was what Freese believed as well, but he soon found out, again, that God had a different idea.

Driving on an ice-covered road one morning in January 2009, Freese's car slid off the road and veered into a ditch. Freese suffered injuries to both lower legs, leaving him on crutches when he should have been going through his final training before heading to Florida and the start of spring training.

That was the beginning of two injury-filled seasons for Freese, who played only seventeen games for the Cardinals in 2009 and sixty-four more at three minor league levels. He underwent three different operations on both ankles in the span of sixteen months, denying him the chance to play when he should have been coming into his prime seasons. Then, in December 2009, came the incident that really forced Freese to reevaluate where he was in his life, and he ended up in his bedroom, asking God for help.

The following spring, Freese knew his life was about to change.

"I firmly believe that God puts things in front of you for a reason," Freese said then. "Sometimes it may not be the best thing in the world, but it's an important test. How I rebound is important. How I rebound, that's how I will be viewed. So far, I'm doing great. I'm real positive, and I'm as confident and ready as I've ever been."

He was in the starting lineup for the Cardinals on opening day in 2010, but Freese should have realized his recovery, both spiritually and physically, was not going to be that easy. A bone bruise on his right ankle sent him to the disabled list in June for two months. Then, playing in his first rehab game, the ankle gave way again, leading to another season-ending injury.

"I definitely didn't make it easy on myself numerous times," Freese said. "You can sit back and think for a while on things I have had to deal with, but you keep plugging away."

All of those efforts finally paid off in a major way when he became the postseason hero in 2011, leading the Cardinals to their eleventh world championship. All that success, however, only set up the next challenge for Freese—to try to put it all behind him as the 2012 season began.

His new manager, Matheny, was confident that Freese was ready for the pressure.

"I know that, with the humble person and player that he is, all the attention really was not what he was hoping for because he realizes he still has a lot to prove in this game," Matheny said, "not necessarily to us, but to himself. I think he knows he wants to be a better defensive player. I know that he wants to put together a more consistent season, and he wants his body to do what it will allow him to do out there as much as possible.

"It's not as if David Freese is content with what has happened and now he is just going to cash in his chips. He's very motivated. He's excited about 2012."

Freese was in the fifth spot in the batting order for opening day in Miami, and he came up in the bottom of the first inning with two outs and runners on second and third. Facing Josh Johnson, he calmly lined a single to left, driving in the first two runs of the season and leading the Cardinals to a 4–1 victory. Freese finished the day with three hits.

He did not downplay the possibility of the 2011 playoff and World Series success carrying over into the new season.

"The playoffs can do wonders for you—learning how to keep your composure and not to get too anxious," Freese said. "If you embrace it and soak in all those postseason experiences, they definitely can help you. You can't run from anything. This game will eat you up if you run from it."

Freese's efforts helped assure that Matheny won his first regular-season game as a manager, and he was one of the ringleaders as the players presented Matheny with the game ball, then showered him with bottles of water while he was standing in the hallway outside his office.

"It was nice to get Mike that first win," Freese said. "In the back of our minds, we wanted to give him that first one right away. . . . He's a special person and he deserved this as soon as possible."

The win began a good stretch for both Freese and the Cardinals. By the end of April, in his first twenty games of the season, Freese had hit 5 homers, driven in 20 runs, and had a .333 batting average. The team was 14–8 in April, and on the morning of May 2, had a four-and-a-half-game lead in the National League Central.

Then came May, and a .211 average, which hit its rock-bottom point on May 20, when, during a Sunday night game at Los Angeles, Freese struck out in all four of his at-bats. He swung and missed on eight pitches.

Freese had always been a player who handled the highs pretty well in his career and life but had struggled with the lows. As the team returned home, he was definitely at a low point.

Matheny gave him two days off for a mental break. Freese celebrated his return to the lineup with a two-run homer but tried to take it in stride as just another game during a long season.

"Sometimes you get in that box and you want to be Superman," Freese said. "That's not going to help you out. You have to stay with your plan and try to execute.

"With that said, you're going to have ups and downs. I think there are a lot of people out there that don't understand that. But in this clubhouse, we know what a season is like and what the game can do to you. You just have to grind it out."

Trying to even out the lows has been a challenge for Freese.

"The lows get me," he said. "Faith gets kicked in, and I wish I was better at that. I know the more you invest in God, the easier the lows become. I think you become stronger. You push through stuff more. When God is inside you, things are easier to deal with. He's going to give you stuff you can handle."

Freese attributes his ability to handle the highs to his parents, who raised him in a Christian environment, something he appreciates now more than he did then.

"I went to church, but probably more on authority than on my choice," Freese said. "I appreciate the fact that my parents are deep in faith. I'm young in faith compared to a lot of people.

"I've had good fortune in my life, to be sure. I had a good childhood. Things have happened that have taught me to be humble. I've learned that tangible things are not what life is all about. If the word *humble* is not in your dictionary, it is going to find you quick."

Freese rebounded from the low of May with another .300 month in June, and in early July, as he was about to walk into the team's weekly Bible study, he found Matheny waiting in the hallway to deliver the news—in front of his teammates—that Freese had won the fan vote for the final spot on the National League All-Star team.

"I wanted to let his teammates experience that moment too," Matheny said. "You stack his numbers up and he's deserving. I'm just excited to see him get that because I imagine the first [All-Star game] is going to be extra special."

Freese was one of five Cardinals to make the All-Star team, joining starters Carlos Beltran and Rafael Furcal, pitcher Lance Lynn, and outfielder Matt Holliday, who was added as a reserve in place of catcher Yadier Molina, who had to decline the invitation because of the death of his wife's grandfather in Puerto Rico.

The voting process for the final roster spot included votes

on Twitter and by text messages, a process that left Freese a little dazed, but still happy and proud.

"What a crazy process," he said, "but the Cardinals organization going out of the way for me and doing everything that they did, it was a huge help."

Becoming an All-Star really was not one of Freese's goals as the 2012 season began, but it did help move him toward his ultimate goal of becoming a complete player.

Really, to him, that was what 2012 was all about. He doesn't want people to look back when his career is over and say he had a good month in October 2011. He wants them to be able to say he had a good, or even great, career.

Which, Freese knows, never would have been possible without his decision to turn his life over to Christ.

Freese knows there are other players on the team who are more outspoken about their religion, and he appreciates their ability to talk about their faith. It is something he is still not as comfortable doing in public, but that might change as he gets older.

"I understand in the Bible that as a Christian you are to go out and preach the Word and push the Word, but I'm more of a guy . . . I have my own relationship with God, and with friends and family who are strong in faith. Matt Holliday is that way too. He likes to love on people, but he doesn't push the Word," Freese said.

"I watch Matt and wonder why he has such great people around him. He says it's because God puts them in his life. He puts himself in a good place."

Trying to be like Matt Holliday, Freese decided a long time ago, is not a bad thing.

And when he does have a bad day, Freese finds calm in reading the Bible. His favorite passage is the Twenty-third Psalm.

"I fight that, to lie in calm waters," he said. "It helps me every day, especially in this profession. That's something I definitely try to do. It's really easy to get caught up in the game during the season, and when you take the time to read the Word, when you close the Bible, you definitely feel a little different than when you opened it."

//

TWO

ADAM WAINWRIGHT

However, I consider my life worth nothing to me; my only aim is to finish
the race and complete the task the Lord Jesus has given me—the task
of testifying to the good news of God's grace.

—Acts 20:24 NIV

Two thousand three hundred sixty-eight nights had passed in
Adam Wainwright's life between October 17, 2005, and April 13,
2012, when Wainwright walked to the bullpen to get ready for his
start in the Cardinals' home opener against the Cubs.

With every step he took that day, Wainwright knew he was
in this position only because of what happened on that October
night six and a half years earlier.

Wainwright was in the family room at his home in St.
Simons, Georgia, that evening, and like all Cardinals fans in St.
Louis and elsewhere, he was watching game five of the National
League Championship Series between the Cardinals and the
Houston Astros.

Wainwright would have liked to have been at Minute Maid
Park in Houston for the game. He had spent the 2005 season
playing for the Cardinals' Triple-A franchise in Memphis, and

when their season was over, he got the call to join the major league club.

Over the final three weeks of the season, Wainwright got into two games, both in relief, with mixed results. In his major league debut on September 11, he worked the ninth inning in a game against the New York Mets and gave up a three-run homer to Victor Diaz. He didn't pitch again until September 23, when he worked a scoreless seventh inning at Milwaukee, which turned out to be his final game of the season.

Even though he knew he would not be eligible to pitch in the playoffs or the World Series, Wainwright had hoped to be able to stay with the team, cheering from the bench or bullpen. That hope disappeared when manager Tony La Russa told Wainwright that was not going to happen—that the pitcher was being sent home.

So Wainwright was watching on television when Albert Pujols hit one of the most famous postseason homers in Cardinals history off Brad Lidge, a ninth-inning shot that brought an immediate hush to the ballpark, cancelled pennant-winning celebrations, and sent the series back to St. Louis for game six. When it was over, after watching all of his would-be teammates jumping up and down and celebrating like they had won the World Series, Wainwright turned off the television.

"I was excited for the Cardinals, but at the same time I was kind of distraught—mentally, physically, spiritually, every aspect of my life," Wainwright said.

After turning off the television, Wainwright walked out to his backyard and got into a small johnboat, paddling out to the middle of a pond. It was after midnight. The night was quiet. The water was calm. For what he estimates was more than an hour, Wainwright sat alone in the boat thinking—about baseball, about himself and his life, about God.

It was an hour, Wainwright says now, that changed his life forever.

Wainwright had been a gifted athlete in high school, a star in football, basketball, and baseball. He credits his older brother Trey for helping him develop his athletic skills from a very early age. Wainwright's father left his mother when he was very young and Trey, seven years older than Adam, became a father figure to him.

"He taught me to play everything with a ball," Adam says now. "From a very early age, the only thing I wanted to be was a baseball player."

Trey built a pitching mound and cage in the family's backyard so Adam could throw whenever he wanted, even if he didn't have a catcher. The family planned dinner around the Atlanta Braves' schedule so Adam could be in front of the television every night watching one of his heroes—Greg Maddux, Tom Glavine, or John Smoltz—pitch for the Braves.

By the time he was a senior in high school, Wainwright had become one of the best prep players in the country. He had a full-ride scholarship waiting for him at Georgia Tech and, going into the amateur draft, Wainwright wasn't sure if he would sign a pro contract or go to college.

That all changed on June 5, when Wainwright became a first-round pick in the 2000 MLB draft, the twenty-ninth over-all selected player, drafted by the Atlanta Braves. There was a major celebration in the Wainwright household. Ten days later, he was on his way to the Gulf Coast League, an eighteen-year-old who thought he knew where he was headed. All the dreams he had as a young boy were coming true. What Wainwright didn't know then, however, was that God had other plans for him, plans that would be revealed in small doses over the next several years.

Growing up, Wainwright had been a regular in church and

Sunday school. Where he was from, a small town in southeast Georgia, people who didn't go to church, in his words, "were weird."

But while Wainwright was there in body, he knows now he really was never there in spirit.

"There were a lot of things I didn't like about church," he said. "The pews were hard. We had to stand up, sit down, then stand back up. The Bible was hard to read. Being a competitor at heart, I decided to make a game out of it. When the pastor got up to give the sermon, I would start counting, just to see how high I could get. I got up to a thousand a few times.

"At the same time I would memorize one or two sections about what the pastor was preaching about, so when my mom asked me what I learned that day I could say, 'He was talking about Moses and the ark' and she would say, 'Oh great, you really listened.'

"Actually what I was was a big fake, a chameleon. I was someone who was acting like something I wasn't, and I got really good at it."

As a youth Wainwright used sports to fill the void of not having a father in his life. That worked for a while, but as he transitioned to professional baseball, Wainwright often felt something was missing in his life, despite the success he was having on the mound.

After getting off to a 4–0 start in the rookie Gulf Coast League, the Braves promoted him to Danville, Virginia, where he finished the 2000 season. Two years in Class A ball followed, one in Macon, Georgia, and one in Myrtle Beach, South Carolina. Wainwright and the Braves both seemed pleased with the progress he was making, even though Wainwright wanted to find a level of consistency that seemed to be missing.

"I still had a lot of doubts," he said. "If I didn't sleep in my lucky burgundy Duckhead shirt the night before I pitched, I had no chance. If I didn't eat Papa John's pizza the night before I pitched, I had no chance. It was ridiculous. Everything had to line up perfectly for me to do well. That was why I didn't do very well."

He spent the 2003 season at Double-A Greenville, the level where organizations usually make the separation between players who are prospects or suspects.

Despite being his own harshest critic, Wainwright was still a good prospect. He pitched well enough, in the opinion of others, to be selected as a prospect sent to the Arizona Fall League as a candidate to make the US team for the 2004 Olympics. He was excited to get the chance to work with Dave Stewart, the former ace of the Oakland Athletics, who was the Olympic team's pitching coach.

Two years later, as he sat in the boat in the middle of the pond behind his house in the chill of that October night, Stewart was one of the people Wainwright thought about.

"When I got in that boat, I started thinking about all the failure I had come across," Wainwright said. "I thought of my Double-A pitching coach telling me I would never make it unless I made some changes. I thought of Dave Stewart."

Wainwright was one of the players sent home from that pre-Olympic team, told by Stewart that he would never make it as a pitcher unless he got mentally tough.

"In my eyes Dave Stewart was one of the best competitors in baseball, and here he was telling me I was not 'mentally tough,'" Wainwright said. "He told me I had no confidence. He told me I didn't believe in myself. I said, 'You don't know what you are talking about.' I was pretty devastated."

After he got back home to Georgia, just as he was preparing to ask his prospective father-in-law for permission to marry his daughter, Wainwright got another blow to his confidence. On December 13, 2003, he learned from a phone call that he had been traded to the Cardinals.

On the boat, Wainwright also thought about that day, and how he later learned one of the reasons he had been traded was because Atlanta manager Bobby Cox and pitching coach Leo Mazzone also had questions about whether he had the makeup to be successful in the major leagues.

Wainwright thought about both of those men that night in 2005, and he thought about La Russa. Mostly, though, he thought about himself.

"I was talking out loud with God. 'If You are really a God, why don't You give me some answers? Why is it, when I am pitching in the minors, I can't figure out anything? Why is it when I pitched for Team USA I was one of the only guys sent home? Why was Dave Stewart saying I would never make it? Why did Bobby Cox and John Schuerholz trade me? Are all of those people crazy?'

"All of those things kept coming around, and finally I realized it wasn't the world's problem; it was my problem. I wasn't the only one who was right and everybody else was wrong. I was the one who was wrong. Everybody else was right. That was a moment of clarity for me.

"It turned out there was somebody else sitting with me in that boat. I said to God, 'From now on, if I am supposed to be a baseball player, I am going to throw every pitch like it's the last pitch I will ever throw. When I come back, I am going to be different.' And that's what I did."

Three years earlier, Wainwright had been a minor league teammate and roommate with pitcher Blaine Boyer, a Christian. At Boyer's invitation, Wainwright attended a conference of Pro Athletes Outreach, a Christian group for professional athletes. He also met a man named Steve Hammond, who would become his agent.

"At the conference there was a speaker who talked about having a relationship with Jesus Christ," Wainwright said. "It was the first time I had heard the word *relationship* associated with Christianity. I felt like God was tapping me on the shoulder. I was asking questions and He was answering them.

"Everybody there had a glow in their eyes. I wanted that glow. I decided to put my faith in God and stop living a lie. It just took me three years to finally do it. That's how embedded the devil and his accomplices are in our brains and in today's society."

La Russa and pitching coach Dave Duncan could see the change in Wainwright as soon as he reported to spring training the following year. He had worked harder than ever before in the off-season, as he had promised God and himself. When he felt lazy, he worked out twice instead, whereas in the past he might have taken a day off.

"I wanted, physically and mentally, to believe I was good enough," he said.

Wainwright would soon get the validation he craved.

"Before I threw one pitch, Dunc said to me, 'You look different,'" Wainwright said.

Duncan asked Wainwright what the difference was and Wainwright said, "Stick around and I will show you."

"Tony later asked me the same thing, and I told him I had figured some things out. I pitched every pitch that year like it was the last pitch of the World Series. When I threw that last pitch of the World Series, it was not a big deal because in my mind I had already done it sixty-two times."

Besides a World Series ring, Wainwright has another memento from that victory over the Detroit Tigers—a painting of him striking out Brandon Inge for the final out.

The artist came to spring training in 2007 trying to sell that painting and several others to the Cardinals players. Wainwright loved the painting, but still being worried about his future, balked at the price, which was five thousand dollars. As Wainwright talked with the artist, Albert Pujols listened in to the conversation. Pujols told Wainwright that he would buy it for him. Wainwright refused, but Pujols told him if he refused again, he was going into the manager's office and telling La Russa to send Wainwright back to Triple-A. Wainwright graciously accepted the gift.

The 2006 season, spent in the bullpen, was the start of a remarkable five-year run of success for Wainwright, who moved into the Cardinals' rotation in 2007 and quickly established himself as one of the best starters in the National League. He led the league with nineteen wins in 2009 and won twenty for the first time the next year.

Having finished third in the Cy Young Award voting in 2009 and second in 2010, Wainwright knew many people were predicting he could win the award in 2011, and he honestly felt he was good enough to do it too. But once again, Wainwright quickly learned that God had another plan in mind for him.

During his first bullpen session in spring training, on the next-to-last pitch he was scheduled to throw, Wainwright blew out his right elbow. The medical diagnosis came quickly—Wainwright would need Tommy John surgery, where a new ligament is transplanted into the elbow, and he would not be able to pitch for the entire season.

"It was my year to be humbled," he said.

Wainwright became one of the team's most vocal cheerleaders, urging on his teammates through one of the most miraculous comebacks in baseball history, all the way to the victory in game seven of the World Series.

He admits the only way he was able to get through the season, and keep his positive outlook, was because of his strong faith. If the injury had happened earlier in his career, that would not have been the case, he confessed.

"I would have handled it 180 degrees differently," Wainwright said. "It's not that I was a bad person before; I was a lost person. I would have been feeling sorry for myself. I don't know if I would have been a complete Debbie Downer all the time, but I certainly would not have been a positive influence.

"I think it's all by design. God is going to use this entire situation for His glory, no matter what the outcome is as far as winning and losing."

Wainwright's positive attitude throughout his recovery and rehab made a difference as he began to throw in earnest in 2012 spring training. If anything, he was ahead of where the doctors expected him to be. He had learned during his year of not pitching how much he loved baseball and how he couldn't wait to get back on the mound.

On April 13, when the Cardinals returned to Busch Stadium to play their home opener against the Chicago Cubs, the rotation was aligned so that Wainwright was on the mound. It had been 571 days since he last pitched a game there, and now he was the returning hero. The start of the game was delayed by rain, but as he walked in from the bullpen before the game, Wainwright received a thunderous standing ovation.

The scene was set, but it would turn out to be what Wainwright later called one of the most disappointing days of his career. He gave up four runs before he could get two outs, and his day was over after the third inning of what ended as a 9–5 victory by the Chicago Cubs.

The eight runs Wainwright allowed equaled the most he had given up in any of his previous 121 major league starts. He apologized to the Cardinals fans, saying, "Today was the perfect storm of horribleness."

Wainwright made a vow to himself and to the fans that he would get better.

"I plan on pitching a lot more games here at Busch Stadium," he said. "There are going to be games where I give up hits. Today was a bad day. I will be better than I was today."

For much of the first two months of the season, as he tried to restore the magic in his right arm, Wainwright went through a lot of ups and downs. He would pitch well, have good results, and then pitch poorly. On May 12, against Atlanta, he walked three batters in a row in one inning—something he had never done before in his career.

Wainwright was trying to get back the command of his fastball, to get the life on the ball that gave it such important movement as it reached home plate. His curveball was good, but he couldn't use it as he wanted without his good fastball. His velocity was okay too, but as with all aspects of his performance, it wasn't quite where he wanted it to be.

That all changed on the night of May 22, in a start against the San Diego Padres, when everything Wainwright had been working on finally came together. The result was a 4–0 four-hitter, the third shutout of his career, and the win brought out a string of emotions from Wainwright. As he hugged catcher Yadier Molina near the mound after the game's final out, Wainwright had to fight back tears. He had already won a lot of games in his career, and had thrown many important and meaningful pitches, but this night was different.

"I think that might be the best feeling I've ever had pitching," Wainwright said after the game. "I've done some things that were pretty fun, but I can't ever remember feeling that emotional after a game. It was a different, more personal level. Today was pretty special."

When Wainwright retired Jesús Guzmán for the game's final out, he let out what he described as a "girly" yell.

"It was a huge sense of relief, a huge sense of feeling blessed," he said. "I've worked very hard to get back to where I am. It was acknowledgment to the hard work.

"I think all of the emotion came from just knowing that it's been over a year since I've done that, since I've felt that locked in on the mound. Mentally, tonight I was so much better than I have been. This year it started kind of rough for me but I knew if I kept grinding it would come back. Now I've kind of set the bar, so I want to make sure I'm locked in like that and focused like that every game."

The ball from the final out of the game sat in the chair in front of Wainwright's locker as he spoke to reporters, ready for him to take it home for a spot on the mantel.

That performance, more than anything else, let Wainwright know that he was now past the point where he had to worry about his arm. If there had been doubts about how well he would pitch after the surgery, they were now gone. There was now no reason, Wainwright knew, why he could not expect to pitch every game like he had pitched during the 2009 and 2010 seasons.

There would still be ups and downs, yes, as there are for every pitcher in every season. Through the middle of the year, Wainwright was still losing as many games as he was winning. He had a 7–8 record at the All-Star break, and opened the second half by losing consecutive starts at Cincinnati and Milwaukee. Against the Brewers, three unearned runs were the difference as he struck out nine, did not walk a batter, and allowed only four hits.

It was the final game of a 1–5 road trip that dropped the Cardinals four and a half games out of first place. Wainwright spoke up after the game, telling reporters he didn't believe the team was playing with the sense of urgency that was needed.

Maybe he decided to lead by example. Wainwright went 3–0 in his next four starts, allowing just six earned runs in 29 1/3 innings, as he evened his season record at 10–10.

More important to him was the fact the Cardinals were playing better as a team, displaying more life as they tried to chase down the Reds and Pirates in the National League Central and wild-card race.

After beating the Brewers 6–1 on August 4, with a complete-game four-hitter, Wainwright acknowledged that it was nice to finally see the day when he knew what to expect as he went to the mound, game in and game out.

"I never gave up hope, even though I wasn't pitching nearly like I wanted to," he said. "I wasn't executing like I wanted to, the stuff wasn't good. But I knew if I kept grinding, it would eventually get there. It took me close to two months to really feel good on the mound, and ever since then I've felt great."

Before that game, as he does every time he is going to pitch, Wainwright sets aside time to pray before he heads to the bullpen to begin his warm-up.

"I pray for strength. I pray that God would sharpen my mind, strengthen my body," Wainwright said. "Usually there's a theme. I kind of look at how David prays in Psalms. He's praying sometimes 'let my enemies turn to dust,' sometimes he's praying 'why this or why that,' or sometimes he is just praising God. But I always pray for a strong body and sharp mind.

"I try to make a habit of praying at least once a day without asking for anything, just praising God."

Wainwright, who believes his prayers were answered during his 14–13 season, in which he was able to make thirty-two starts, knows it is far more common for people to turn to God when they are in a crisis, or when their lives are in turmoil, but he knows that God wants to share in the successes just as much as He is there to help people through their troubles.

"There's always things you question God about," Wainwright said. "I don't think there is anything wrong with that. That was the way David lived. He was in constant dialogue with God and crying out to God, asking why and praising God. Throughout our struggles I think it's okay to ask God why things are happening. There's nothing wrong with asking why. I continue to talk to God.

"It's not okay to play God and think He is turning His back on you."

Wainwright has learned over the years that baseball is a game where individuals are going to fail more than they succeed. He believes God understands life is like that too.

"We are called to live our lives the way Jesus would all the time, and we fail at it most of the time," Wainwright said. "The key is to try to. Trying doesn't mean trying to go out and do great acts to please God. You love God, and therefore you want to go out and do things that would please Him.

"Hopefully that's reflected by the way I do things. Sometimes you need to be up front about what you believe and other times you lead by example. I once heard a great quote: 'Preach the gospel every day, and sometimes use words.' That just speaks to the life you live."

Wainwright knows one of the blessings he has received is to have a manager like Mike Matheny, who also is a strong Christian, and to be joined by so many teammates who have the same beliefs.

"It's much easier to get together when it doesn't need to be a secret," he said. "I think you have a chance to play better when you are open with your teammates and when you bond with your teammates. When you are close with guys, you really root for people. There is nobody in this clubhouse who is out there selfishly wanting other people to do badly. This is a team that really wants others to do well and really cares for each other.

"The chemistry in this clubhouse has gotten better and better each year that I've been here, definitely."

That strong bond exists not only among the players but also

among everybody who works inside that clubhouse. When someone in the family is hurting, everyone feels the pain.

Wainwright thinks that some people have the misconception that being a Christian makes someone weak. Nothing, he said, could be further from the truth, and anybody who has seen Wainwright on the mound can attest to that.

"I can tell you, from experience, and other people will tell you too, that being a believer does not make you weak," he said. "Jesus is described in the Bible as meek, not weak. Meek is strength under control. When we have the good Lord, who has created this entire world and is all-knowing, omnipotent, and omnipresent, we have a source of strength that a nonbeliever can't tap into.

"We have a gift of freedom given to us because we know where we are going, we know who we are living for, and why we are living the way we do. It gives us peace and freedom. There's tools that you take from Christianity that make you much stronger than you would be otherwise."

THREE

RIP ROWAN

For God so loved the world, that he gave his only begotten Son, that whosoever believeth in him should not perish, but have everlasting life.

—John 3:16 KJV

Rip Rowan began working for the Cardinals on a part-time basis in 1977, as the batboy for whichever team was visiting Busch Stadium. Rowan's father was a painter who worked at the stadium, and he found out about the opening through his friendship with other club employees. By the start of the next season, Rowan had a full-time job with the team.

Thirty-five years later, Rowan still works for the Cardinals and has never worked anywhere else. After giving up the batboy job after a couple of years, he worked in the visiting team's clubhouse, and as an assistant in the home clubhouse until 2003, when he assumed the title of equipment manager.

Rowan does not take his position lightly, knowing that he is only the third person to hold this job in the last eighty years. Butch Yatkeman basically created the position in the 1920s and worked until 1983, when Buddy Bates took over and did it for the next twenty seasons.

Rowan is one of the people who works behind the scenes, making certain that the uniforms get cleaned every day, that the clubhouse is orderly, and that the players have all the equipment they need to do their jobs on the field. He is the type of employee who largely is taken for granted by many until something out of the ordinary occurs.

On the afternoon of May 3, 2012, the Cardinals lost 6–3 to the Pittsburgh Pirates at Busch Stadium. It was a getaway day—the team was completing a home stand and heading for Houston to begin a six-game trip to play the Houston Astros and Arizona Diamondbacks. Getaway days are always the busiest days for Rowan, who must make certain all the players' equipment, personal belongings, and training supplies get from one city to the next.

Because he has been doing this job for ten years, Rowan has the schedule down to a science. He knows what time the team bus will be leaving the ballpark to head for the airport, and he knows he needs to have all the equipment and other items loaded on the rental truck so he can leave in the truck a few minutes ahead of the team bus. That way, he can be loading the equipment onto the charter flight as the players, coaches, and other personnel arrive, helping ensure the team does not have a long delay before the flight is ready for takeoff.

The team bus usually leaves about an hour after the game, and on May 3, the bus was leaving at 5:05 p.m. That meant Rowan wanted the equipment truck loaded and headed for the airport shortly before 5:00 p.m.

"It was a Thursday afternoon, and it's always hit and miss because of the traffic," said Rowan, knowing it is normally about a fifteen-minute drive from Busch Stadium to Lambert Airport. "I try to leave about seven or eight minutes ahead of the bus."

Rowan has never encountered more than minor problems in his ten years of performing the job, but as he sat in the passenger seat of the rental truck that day, just leaving down-town, he could see the traffic on Interstate 70 ahead was already stopped.

The driver, who worked for the rental truck company, saw the same traffic at the same time as Rowan.

"We were in the fast lane, and he kind of veered to the left toward the shoulder," Rowan said. "He was doing it out of instinct, but that made me more vulnerable on the passenger side. I saw that we were going to hit the back of a stopped SUV."

As the truck slammed into the back of the SUV, the impact pushed the truck engine backward, and the truck's dashboard collapsed into the passenger seat. Rowan was trapped from his waist down.

"I realized I was trapped immediately," Rowan said. "The driver was in kind of a panic mode. I told him to go check on the other vehicles to make sure everyone was okay and to call 9-1-1. He said he had never been in an accident before, and it was almost like I was having to try to calm him down.

"His main concern was for me. The impact of the crash had thrown me into the windshield, which was busted out. Even though I was trying to calm him down, I was scared and nervous. I knew I was trapped, and the first thing that came to my mind was 'Good Lord, don't let this thing catch fire.' I didn't know what I was going to do if something happened."

At about the same time the police arrived, the bus carrying the Cardinals players and personnel to the airport passed the accident. Realizing it was their equipment truck, the bus stopped on the side of the highway and manager Mike Matheny and train-ers Greg Hauck and Chris Conroy got out and came up to the truck to see if there was anything they could do to help.

Everyone, including the police officers, could do nothing but wait for paramedics and the fire department to arrive so they could use the Jaws of Life to open up the cab of the truck and get Rowan out of the vehicle.

"Greg kept asking me questions about, 'Could I move my feet?' or, 'Could I feel my toes,'" Rowan said. "I said I was fine but I just needed to get out of there. I was just hoping somebody would pull me out of there soon. I just wanted out.

"I didn't think I was that badly hurt, but anxiety was starting to set in. I was real apprehensive, but I didn't feel pain. Mike and the guys were trying to calm me down and tell me not to worry, that the fire department would be there soon. At one point I told Greg to go get some guys off the bus and pull this sucker off me. He said they couldn't do that, but that if the truck caught fire and was burning they would have gotten me out.

"I had so many thoughts going through my head. It probably was about fifteen minutes until the fire department got there, but it seemed like it was weeks."

Once Rowan was cut out of the vehicle, he was carried to a waiting ambulance. Assured that he was going to be okay, Matheny and the rest of the team left and headed on to the airport. Ernie Moore, the team's assistant equipment manager, made sure the equipment was loaded onto another truck and then onto the airplane, and he accompanied the team to Houston.

It was about that time when Rowan realized he might have been more seriously hurt than he had thought.

"I didn't feel pain when I was trapped," he said. "I didn't feel pain until I got in the ambulance. The doctors told me later that was all because of adrenalin."

The doctors also told Rowan that he was experiencing a great deal of swelling in his legs, the result of having been trapped so long.

"The swelling was the doctor's main concern," Rowan said. "I had what they called compartment syndrome, and they have to open you up to relieve the pressure. I found out that, in some cases, victims had to have their leg or legs amputated."

The doctors did not believe Rowan was suffering from that severe of a case, but they wanted him to remain hospitalized overnight for observation.

"I didn't look at my leg at the hospital, but one of the team doctors told me it had swelled up pretty big," Rowan said.

That night, in his hospital room, Rowan thanked God that he had lived through the accident and had not been more seriously injured. He has continued to thank God every day since.

"It could have been a lot worse," Rowan said. "If I had not seen it coming, I might have crashed harder into the windshield and cut up my face instead of hitting it with my arm. There's some reason there. I could have been really messed up. I'm very thankful that it wasn't worse, because it could have been horrible."

As is the case with anybody who goes through an accident like that, it prompted Rowan to assess his life and what was truly important to him. His highest priorities, even more so now, are his family and his faith.

Rowan was in the hospital for only one night, going home the next afternoon to his young son and his wife, Courtney, who was expecting their second child. (He also has two older boys from a previous marriage.) Rowan rested at home while the Cardinals were out of town, but when the team returned to Busch Stadium on May 11, Rowan was back at work.

"I still had a lot of swelling in my right leg and ankle," Rowan said. "I was not maneuvering too well."

So Rowan stayed home from the Cardinals' next road trip as well, a five-day trek to California. Doctors recommended that he not fly until the swelling in his leg had decreased, but by May 21, eighteen days after the accident, Rowan was back to work full-time.

Even though he has recovered from his injuries, Rowan knows he will forever be changed because of the accident.

"For one thing, I wear a seat belt every time I get in a car or truck now," he said. "I have to admit I wasn't wearing one the day of the accident. I get scared easier now when we get in a car, and I'm always kind of jumpy. When something like that happens, it just makes you a little more conscious of what's going on around you."

As much as he likes and appreciates his job, part of what Rowan began to question after the accident was how many more years he wants to put in the long hours and weeks of travel that the job requires.

For a normal 7:00 p.m. home game, Rowan arrives at Busch Stadium no later than noon. Following the game, he and his crew will work for a couple of hours, making each day about a twelve-hour workday. For road games, he usually leaves the hotel at 1:00 p.m. for a 7:00 p.m. game, and gets back to the hotel close to midnight.

"I'm at the top position I'm going to have," Rowan said. "I'm not going to go anywhere else. I'll do this until I retire. It's a great job with great benefits, and everybody with the Cardinals has always been great to me. Everybody I know looks at it like, 'You work for the Cardinals—how great can that be?'

"I've met a lot of great people in this job and I work for great people. They have been wonderful to me. I'm very fortunate and blessed to have what I have."

FOUR

LANCE BERKMAN

How can a young man cleanse his way?
By taking heed according to Your word.
With my whole heart I have sought You;
Oh, let me not wander from Your commandments!
Your word I have hidden in my heart,
That I might not sin against You.

—Psalm 119:9–11 NKJV

On the morning of May 25, as he was administered anesthesia to prepare for yet another operation on his right knee, Lance Berkman went to sleep not knowing if he would be able to play baseball when he woke up.

He was at peace with whatever would happen.

Berkman had no way of knowing how extensive the surgery would be. It was possible that, for the second time in his career, he had torn his ACL a week earlier during a game at Dodger Stadium. If that turned out to be the case, doctors were prepared to transplant a ligament from his leg to his knee, a decision that would probably bring an end to Berkman's outstanding career.

This was the fifth knee surgery Berkman had undergone

during his career, the third on his right knee. If the ACL was indeed torn, Berkman—at age thirty-six—honestly didn't know if he would want to go through all of the rehab necessary to continue playing baseball.

"I realize I can't play baseball forever, and I don't want to play baseball forever," Berkman said. "That's something which might surprise some people, because on the outside looking in, playing baseball is great, and there are aspects of it that are tremendous. But it's definitely not something I want to do forever.

"When the end of my career comes, I will be perfectly fine with it. If the knee injury had happened a year or two into my career, it might have been a different deal, but because of what I have been able to accomplish and the position I'm in in my life right now, I was perfectly at peace with whatever happened physically."

When he awoke in the Houston recovery room, Berkman quickly learned the injury was not as extensive as first feared. The ACL was not damaged. Doctors repaired a torn meniscus and frayed cartilage. The prognosis: he would be able to play again in six to eight weeks. It was about the most positive outcome there could have been.

Up to that point, the season had been a frustrating one for Berkman, as he had missed more games with injuries than he had played. A left calf strain limited him to just seven at-bats between April 10 and May 12, and he had played only five games before he was injured again in the game on May 19.

It would have been understandable for any player, even one as naturally optimistic as Berkman, to become frustrated, upset, and bitter about what quickly was turning into a lost season. It was Berkman's strong faith in God, however, that kept that from happening.

Every aspect of Berkman's life is driven and directed by his faith, and baseball is only part of what defines him. Playing baseball is what he does, but his roles as husband, father, friend, and Christian are what truly matter.

"Faith is not a tool," he said. "It's a way of life. It's the way you look at everything. It's not like a pair of spectacles that you take on and off. It's just who you are. It's what you become. It helps keep everything in perspective and [influences] the way you view the game.

"To a lot of people, this game is a religion. I watched a lot of the Hall of Fame ceremonies, and people were just batty about it. I don't want to take away from a lifetime achievement and the acknowledgment of such because it is important, but to worship at the shrine of that is a little ridiculous. Faith helps you keep things like that in perspective."

That's a lesson Berkman has learned throughout his baseball career and his life, since his days growing up in Texas. Raised in a Christian household, Berkman really didn't establish his own relationship with Christ until he was a student at Rice University.

"When you grow up in a household of faith, it's not an uncommon experience for you to adopt the faith of your family," Berkman said. "You grow up with certain habits and traditions, not necessarily your own, until you embrace them when you get out on your own. That was what it was like for me in college.

"I had a good foundation, but I didn't really kind of 'own' my faith until I was in college. That's when you are thinking for yourself for the first time. If you don't want to go to church, you don't have to go to church. That period of my life is where I found my faith for myself, instead of just regurgitating the way I was brought up."

At Rice, Berkman met a man who was instrumental in helping him develop that relationship with Christ. His name was Jake Baker, a teammate on the Rice baseball team. Baker also became important to Berkman for more personal reasons—Lance later married Baker's sister, Cara.

"I definitely feel like the Lord used him to kind of get my attention, to get me going in the right path," Berkman said.

The strong foundation of his faith helped Berkman in numerous ways as he broke into professional baseball and then became a star with the Houston Astros.

"My faith has been tested from the standpoint of trying not to put too much attention on your performance in the game," he said. "Too much weight is placed on the money you can make, the fame that comes with it. Maintaining the proper mentality is a test; not a test of faith, because you still believe in God, but the principles and the way that God expects you to act—that can be tested."

What Berkman quickly realized once he made it to the major leagues was that he was given the ability by God to be able to play major league baseball. Doing that brought with it a certain responsibility and obligation to use that platform to glorify God, something he has always tried to do.

"Everybody has a responsibility to God, in my opinion, for the abilities they have been given," Berkman said. "Everybody has a platform. Everybody has the opportunity. Just because I'm a professional baseball player, I might have a bigger platform because of a public status, but everybody can have an impact on the people they are around—their families, coworkers—no matter what you do.

"The beauty is in the example of Jesus Christ. If you read the gospel, He didn't go to the famous people or the popular people. He went to the prostitutes, the tax collectors, lepers—the scum of the earth, so to speak—and He used them. Everybody—I don't care who you are—has an opportunity to respond to God and engage with God in such a way that it comes out in your life and impacts the people they come in contact with, the people they are around daily."

For Berkman, that group is primarily his teammates. It didn't take him long after signing with the Cardinals as a free agent in 2011 to become the spiritual and motivational leader of the team. It was a role pitcher Adam Wainwright knew Berkman would inherit because of what he knew of Berkman through their relationship in Pro Athletes Outreach, and what he had seen of him as an opponent with the Houston Astros. Berkman's relationship with Wainwright, and with other Christian players on the Cardinals, made the Cardinals an easy choice for him when he knew he would not re-sign with the Astros.

"One of the things that really was attractive to me about this organization is they had a lot of guys who I knew had a good understanding of what the gospel is all about," Berkman said. "It's always nice to play and compete with guys who feel and believe the same way you do."

Berkman watched as that group of players grew stronger in their faith between the 2011 and 2012 seasons.

"We've got some young guys who were less mature in their faith last year and they continue to grow and learn, so that makes for a stronger group," he said. "We're all a year farther down the road."

As sort of an elder-statesman on the team, Berkman is often approached for advice by younger players—about the game, about an aspect of faith, or just about being a husband and father and dealing with problems that come up because of the pressures inherent in their chosen occupation. He is comfortable and happy to talk to anyone about any of those topics.

"It's not like I'm sitting on top of a mountain, cross-legged, waiting for people to come up to me," Berkman said. "We certainly have discussions in our Bible studies and chapel time. We talk amongst each other. If I have a strong feeling about something or an experience that I think can benefit the group, I will share it.

"To me the baseball talk is secondary. The opportunity to speak and get into guys' lives and help on a personal level any way I can is far more important than professionally."

One of the young players who leaned on Berkman for advice was Matt Carpenter, another Texas native who grew up watching Berkman play for the Astros when he was in high school. In 2012, his locker was adjacent to Berkman's in the Cardinals' clubhouse.

"Lance, in my opinion, and I'm sure everybody else would be on board, is the most knowledgeable guy when it comes to the Bible that I've ever been around who wasn't an actual pastor," Carpenter said. "He has an incredible amount of knowledge. I love picking his brain."

The search for knowledge has always motivated Berkman, who was drafted in the first round by the Astros after his junior season at Rice, where he jokes he was majoring in "eligibility."

Since college he has taken a few theology and Bible-based courses from the College of Biblical Studies–Houston. He has not pursued an advanced degree but has still reaped the benefit of taking the classes. He also intends to one day go back to Rice to complete his undergraduate degree.

"I like to read," Berkman said. "I don't consider myself to be a brilliant person, but I do enjoy the learning process. I enjoy knowing things and exploring things. It's something I'm really interested in, and is a good way to develop my mind and increase my knowledge."

As he continues to study and learn from the Bible, Berkman has become even more amazed at people who fail to understand the principles laid out there and the impact they can have on a person's daily life.

"To me, from the inside looking out, it's obvious," he said. "If people doubt the Bible, I say, 'Just live how it says for a while and tell me if your life is not better because of it.' It will be. The flip side of that is, look at all of the broken families we have, and the other problems we have in society with the people who live without a moral foundation. 'How is life working out for you?'

"It's not a cure-all because there are still good Christian people that bad things happen to, but the more you live your life from the principles in the Bible, the happier your life is in the here and now, not just after you die. It's the way to live your life, and the people who disagree with that, I challenge them to do it and see what happens."

One person who understands that is former Cardinals pitcher Todd Worrell, now the president of the St. Louis chapter of the Fellowship of Christian Athletes, who assists the current team with Bible study and chapel.

"Christians live in the same world as everybody else," Worrell said. "Christian people get cancer and die. I read a book one time, and the writer made an analogy that when an area gets hail, everyone gets hailed on. The Christians aren't pushed off to one side. It's not hailing only on the nonbelieving world. Some people kind of think that way."

In one sense, that has happened to Berkman in his career. His faith has not kept him from repeatedly suffering knee injuries, knocking him out of a good portion of the 2010 season, and then again severely limiting his playing time in 2012, a year he was looking forward to after helping the Cardinals win the 2011 World Series.

After he recovered from the injury he suffered in May, working hard to get back in the lineup, Berkman suffered another blow when he was hit on the same knee by a pitch by Clayton Kershaw of the Dodgers on July 24. It turned out he needed another operation in August, and he would bat only twenty-two more times during the season, getting only three hits.

Relying on his faith to get through those tough times has been a constant for Berkman, who also cites it as one of the reasons the 2011 Cardinals were able to come back from such a huge deficit and make the playoffs in the regular season, then go on to their postseason success.

While some people think being a Christian makes someone less competitive and less intense, Berkman thinks the complete opposite is true.

"The people who feel you compromise your competitiveness because of your beliefs just don't get it," he said. "They don't understand what being a Christian is really all about. God says you should do everything as unto the Lord, and that means everything to the best of your ability. That means compete as hard as you can compete.

"Guys who are Christians should actually play harder. They should care more and do more. You are trying to maximize the gifts that God has given you. Rather than being a detriment, I think it's a huge benefit because it impacts a guy's play, his approach to the game, and it really impacts a guy when things get tough.

"If you don't have something you can lean on, it's easy to fold up shop. I think last year part of what we were able to accomplish was because we had a lot of believers on the team, guys with high character, guys who are not going to quit no matter what, and you saw the results of that. It doesn't always work out like it did last year, but I think we don't get to where we were without God in this clubhouse."

Ultimately, Berkman and his Christian teammates don't believe that God influences which team wins or loses a baseball game. If one team's best pitcher, a Christian, is on the mound facing another team's best hitter, also a Christian, how is God going to pick who succeeds and who fails? He doesn't.

"I know God cares more about people's souls, the way they are caring for their families," Berkman said. "Who wins and loses a baseball game is irrelevant, I think, in terms of the grand scheme."

Because he is such a student of the Bible, Berkman has many favorite passages. One is Proverbs 16:9, which says, "The mind of man plans his way, but the LORD directs his steps" (NASB).

His interpretation of that passage, particularly in relation to how his 2012 season went, is that even though Berkman was expecting to have another good, injury-free season with the Cardinals, God had other plans for him.

In a column written for the Cardinals' monthly team magazine, Berkman said, "We can have all these grand ideas about what we're going to do and what we can do, but the reality is, it's God that directs and guides us. So if His will for my life is different than what I perceive my will for my life is, I want His will to win out—and it does."

Berkman knows there is a reason, even though he may not learn what it is until much later, why he suffered so many injuries during the 2012 season. He knows it was part of God's plan for his life—just as it was when he met his wife, when the Astros drafted him, and when he signed with the Cardinals.

Overcoming obstacles is nothing new for Berkman. One story he likes to tell about getting past hurdles is the story Jesus told about the wise and foolish builders, contained in the gospels of both Matthew and Luke:

Everyone therefore who hears these words of mine, and does them, I will liken him to a wise man, who built his house on a rock. The rain came down, the floods came, and the winds blew, and beat on that house; and it didn't fall, for it was founded on the rock. Everyone who hears these words of mine, and doesn't do them will be like a foolish man, who built his house on the sand. The rain came down, the floods came, and the winds blew, and beat on that house; and it fell—and great was its fall (Matt. 7:24–27 WEB).

As Berkman points out, the moral of the story is that a person's foundation is the most important aspect of what happens when a storm hits. People without that solid foundation—having built their homes on things contrary to God, such as money, power, and fame—will be in trouble. But someone whose home was built on solid ground—faith in God—will be able to weather whatever storms come his way. Berkman has seen countless examples of both happen to teammates and others in baseball during his playing career.

So instead of moping and bemoaning his fate throughout 2012, Berkman was constantly upbeat, encouraging his teammates, telling jokes and stories to lighten the mood. That role was much easier, Berkman said, because of the other players on the team who shared his beliefs and realized all of the blessings they had been given, including the God-given ability to hit or throw a baseball.

"The baseball locker room is a microcosm of the world," Berkman said. "You meet different people and there are different flavors. The ability to communicate to different kinds of people is God-given, I think. Something I try to incorporate is that you can't paint with a broad brush. Everybody is different. They are going to think about things differently.

"There are certain things, immutables if you will, that I tell guys in group settings: 'Look, this is what God expects of you and this is the way you should be living, and if you are not doing it you should analyze where you are and make an adjustment.'

"A lot of times you're not going to realize the fruits of your labors, if you will, on this side of the grave. But we are called as Christians to live our [lives] in a way that is a good example and good witness to other people, to help as many people as we can, sometimes not even realizing that we are doing it."

Berkman knows that his experience over the previous dozen years taught him many lessons about how to handle his injury-filled 2012.

"It's like being caught in a stream," he said. "The longer you are in it, the more you recognize what God is doing and the opportunities that He puts in front of you. There are moments in my career that have really shaped me as a person. One of those was the 2010 experience when I was hurt, didn't play well, and got traded. When you get put through the fire and come out the other side, you are a little more refined."

Even before the knee injury that prompted the May 25 operation, Berkman had already been dealing with a left calf strain that kept him out of action for almost a month. He thought he was finally healthy when he returned to the starting lineup on May 13, but it was short-lived. He played in only six games, totaling nineteen at-bats, before having his knee give way as he tried to catch a throw from shortstop Rafael Furcal in the May 19 game at Dodger Stadium.

One of the effects of the injury for Berkman and the Cardinals was that he spent much of his rehab and recovery at his home in Houston, which kept him away from his teammates and the clubhouse environment.

In the forty-seven games he missed between May 20 and July 13, the Cardinals were 24–23, and fell from a one-and-a-half-game lead in the National League Central to third place, two and a half games behind the Reds. Berkman returned to the lineup on July 14, the second game after the All-Star break, but his presence was not enough to prevent the Reds from sweeping the Cardinals in the series. As the team flew to Milwaukee to continue the road trip, manager Mike Matheny didn't realize so many people thought the team's season was over until the flight landed and he saw the in-box for text messages on his cell phone was full. Several players also got the same messages, which prompted Matheny to call a team meeting the following day. The goal was to make certain the players knew the season was far from over.

Berkman knew Matheny was right, and he was one of the players who hoped he could make up for the time he had lost dealing with his leg and knee injuries. He should have expected, however, that the way his season had gone, his injury problems would not be behind him. As he neared the end of the season, Berkman began giving more thought to his future and whether his time in St. Louis—and perhaps his career—could be coming to an end. As had been the case in May, when he didn't know what damage doctors would find in his knee, he was prepared for whatever outcome God directed.

"There's only one thing in life that really matters," Berkman said. "When a person is on his deathbed you don't hear them saying, 'I wish I had made more money.' What they say is, 'I wish I had spent more time with my kids' or, 'I wish I had not gotten divorced four times.'

"People always have regrets. But the joys that people experience at the end of their lives always revolve around people and the relationships they have had in their [lives]. They have either done a good job with that, or not done a good job, and if that is the case, there is regret there. That's where the rubber meets the road in life, with people and how you interact with them."

Berkman was once asked a question: If he had to choose, would he rather be known as a good guy or a good baseball player? The answer, he said, was not even close.

"Don't get me wrong, there is ego involved," he said. "You want to be known as a good baseball player too, but if I had to choose between the two, there is no doubt being a good person, a good husband, and a good father is far more important than anything I accomplish on the baseball field.

"God gave me certain abilities to hit a baseball and be an athlete. I didn't do anything to deserve it. I feel like everything I have is God-given. When you have that perspective, you realize everyone has a calling and everybody has certain gifts and abilities. I'm doing what I was gifted to do.

"Just because I can hit a baseball doesn't make me better than anybody else. The things I can control are how I live my life, the impact I have on my teammates, and the people I'm around on a daily basis. That, to me, is more important than what I do on the field."

FIVE

MATT CARPENTER

"All these I have kept," the young man said. "What do I still lack?"

Jesus answered, "If you want to be perfect, go, sell your possessions and give to the poor, and you will have treasure in heaven. Then come, follow me."

When the young man heard this, he went away sad, because he had great wealth.

Then Jesus said to his disciples, "Truly I tell you, it is hard for someone who is rich to enter the kingdom of heaven. Again I tell you, it is easier for a camel to go through the eye of a needle than for someone who is rich to enter the kingdom of God."

When the disciples heard this, they were greatly astonished and asked, "Who then can be saved?"

Jesus looked at them and said, "With man this is impossible, but with God all things are possible."

—Matthew 19:20–26 NIV

Growing up in Texas, Matt Carpenter was a huge fan of the Houston Astros, and a fan of one player in particular—first baseman Lance Berkman.

For his sixteenth birthday, Carpenter's high school girlfriend, who later became his wife, gave him a special present—a Berkman jersey to hang in his bedroom. As fate would have it, years later Berkman and Carpenter saw their lives intertwine when the Cardinals drafted Carpenter in 2009 and Berkman signed with the team as a free agent prior to the 2011 season. The two met in spring training, and Carpenter told Berkman about the jersey.

"I said, 'Oh, great, now you make me feel real old,'" said Berkman, who is ten years Carpenter's senior. "I tell you what, I'm flattered. That's an honor to have that."

After their brief spring training encounter, Carpenter did not get to spend much time with Berkman until the 2012 season began. Carpenter made his major league debut in 2011, but was only with the Cardinals for a couple of weeks before returning to Triple-A. Not sure of where he fit in with the Cardinals when spring training began in 2012, Carpenter was determined to work as hard as possible, and to do as much as possible, to show the organization he was ready to play at the major league level.

There were not many days during the spring when manager Mike Matheny failed to mention how impressed he was with Carpenter and how hard he was working to win a spot as one of the team's utility players—Carpenter was taking ground balls all over the infield and staying on the field when the pitchers took batting practice so he could shag flies in the outfield. That was by design, said Carpenter, who had been primarily a third baseman coming up through the minors and in his high school and college career at Texas Christian University.

"I sat home in October and watched the playoffs and World Series and saw David Freese do some amazing things," Carpenter said. "From a career standpoint, I thought it would be foolish to come to spring training and say I was going to compete for the third-base job. That was not going to happen. He's a great player. It just didn't make sense.

"I thought, if I have any chance of making the team, I had to find another way, so I pretty much worked out at every position except third. I tried to show the coaching staff that I could do some other things. Slowly and surely it worked itself out."

Carpenter's presence became of much greater importance to the Cardinals during the first two months of the season, when Allen Craig was still rehabbing from off-season knee surgery and Berkman was out with a variety of leg and knee injuries. Carpenter started twenty-three of the Cardinals' first forty-two games during the first two months of the 2012 season. As fate would have it, on May 23, two days before Berkman underwent his knee operation, Carpenter himself had to go on the disabled list with a strained oblique, which would force him to miss the next month. While he had never had to deal with an injury at the major league level before, Carpenter did have a history of coming back from injury—a process he now says led him to make a much stronger commitment to Christ.

Carpenter was the son of a high school coach, so playing baseball was always one of the most important aspects of his young life. His goal, as it is with almost every Little Leaguer who falls in love with the game, was to make it to the major leagues. It seemed as if he was on his way when he earned a scholarship to Texas Christian University, and by the time he became a junior, he was looking forward to the amateur baseball draft, signing a contract, and beginning life as a professional. As Carpenter found out, however, that was not the immediate plan God had for his life.

"I was lucky enough to be raised in a Christian home, and I actually was baptized when I was twelve," Carpenter said. "I said I was a Christian, but when I went off to college, I kind of became a normal college student and made a lot of bad decisions, selfish decisions. In baseball I became very lazy in what I was doing."

In the fall of his junior year, Carpenter began feeling some pain in his right arm, near his elbow, as the team went through its off-season workouts.

"The arm was barking a little bit when I went home for Christmas break," Carpenter said. "When we got started practicing in January, it was really killing me. I knew something was wrong. I played the first eight games of the season, and the coach moved me to first base because I couldn't make the throw from third. Eventually it just became unbearable."

More trips to the doctor revealed that Carpenter had torn a ligament in his elbow and would need to undergo surgery—the Tommy John procedure usually performed on pitchers, where a ligament is transferred into a player's elbow. The surgery meant that Carpenter would miss the rest of the season. That development, in turn, meant that Carpenter would not be selected in the amateur draft.

Carpenter remembers the day that the TCU coach, Jim Schlossnagle, called him into his office following the surgery to discuss his future.

"He sat me down and started talking to me," Carpenter said. "He was talking about the baseball side, but I was hearing it from a totally different angle. He told me there were two ways I could go about the injury. I could sit around and pout about it and go through the motions with the rehab and be lazy and come back and be an okay player, finish off my career at TCU, and go get a job and be mediocre.

"Or, he said, you can get after it. You can attack this rehab and get yourself in shape and come back as strong as you possibly can and finish your career off on a great note and see what happens at the next level.

"When he said that I thought to myself, *That's for me.* More than anything else, I wanted to change my life and stop going through the motions in my life and see how far I could get. I wanted to see if I could get everything else in my life in order, and then I thought baseball would take care of itself."

Carpenter has no doubt that his meeting with the coach, and his reaction to it, was orchestrated by God as the jump-start he needed to start living his life the way God intended, and to be able to reap the benefits of that plan.

"That was kind of the awakening moment for me," Carpenter said. "I knew I was living my life in a way that I was not supposed to be doing. That was the moment where I decided to get back in the Word and got back to living how I was supposed to live and get back to doing what I was supposed to be doing.

"It's no coincidence that that was when my career kind of took off. There is no question in my mind that I would not be where I am today if that had not happened. Everything I went through that year was for a reason."

While other parts of his life changed for the good right away, the baseball side of Carpenter's world took a little longer to develop. He had to rehab his elbow following the surgery, earning a medical redshirt that gave him an extra year of eligibility.

He was not drafted after what should have been his senior season. But thanks to the medical redshirt he was able to have a fifth year in college, which not only helped him finish his degree in communications but also gave him more of an opportunity to show scouts he was fully recovered and worth taking a chance on when the draft came.

Carpenter raised his batting average at TCU from .283 in 2008 to .333 with 11 homers, 23 doubles, and 6 triples in 58 games, driving in 47 runs. The Horned Frogs finished the year one game shy of a trip to Omaha for the College World Series. Despite that success, Carpenter knew some teams would be reluctant to take a chance on a fifth-year senior because of his age (he was twenty-three) in a draft populated by teenagers. Carpenter prayed that it would work out, and that some team would give him that chance. All he wanted was the opportunity to show what he could do.

The Cardinals took that chance, using their pick in the thirteenth round. Carpenter was the 399th overall selection in the 2009 draft.

By the end of the 2009 season, which didn't start for Carpenter until the end of June, he had already moved up three levels in the Cardinals' farm system, reaching high Class A Palm Beach. He spent most of 2010 at Double-A Springfield, where he was selected as the organization's minor league player of the year.

While he was having success, Carpenter also was relying on his faith to help carry him through the slumps and disappointing days that are a reality for anybody who plays the game.

"Baseball, in general, is a game of failure," Carpenter said. "If you live and die only with your success in this game, or any tangible thing, you are just never going to be happy. There are too many ups and downs. You can go a week or even a month without getting a hit. Having faith is the only way I can possibly imagine living life and also playing this game."

His success in 2010 earned him a spring training invitation to the major league camp, where Carpenter got to experience firsthand the strong Christian foundation of the team.

"It surprised me, and I was blown away," Carpenter said. "It was so incredible to see and was so exciting to see what strong Christians these guys were. They had a Bible study set up and all of the minor leaguers were invited. They provided food and child care. It was unbelievable.

"These guys were some of the best players and leaders of the team. It definitely was a big deal to me, and encouraged me to see how incredible these guys were."

One of the happiest days of Carpenter's baseball life came on June 3, 2011, when he got the call to join the Cardinals. He made his major league debut at Busch Stadium the following day, starting at third base.

His first at-bat resulted in a groundout to the second baseman, but in the ninth inning Carpenter collected his first major league hit, a double off of Kerry Wood.

It turned out that Carpenter's stay in the major leagues was a brief ten days—he was returned to Memphis on June 14 and spent the rest of the season in the Triple-A club. That double turned out to be his only hit in fifteen at-bats during his stay with the Cardinals.

"I was really disappointed in myself," Carpenter said. "I was not so much disappointed by the fact I went 1-for-15 as I was just the way I felt mentally. I'm not embarrassed to say it now that I got a little overwhelmed and wrapped up with all of the things that go around being in the major leagues and being in that clubhouse.

"Knowing what I know now, I would have gone about it a different way. Things like providing tickets for your family and friends, all the text messages and phone calls, all the things that come with the territory. I let it overwhelm me, and I lost focus of what I was actually doing and the reason why I was there."

As he thought about that period later, Carpenter knew if he got a second chance he would be a much different person. That knowledge, plus watching the Cardinals' World Series run in October, sent him into the off-season more determined than ever before.

"I was extremely motivated last winter," he said. "I told my parents and other family members that my mind-set was going to be on my job. As much as I love my family, and not being rude about it, I let them know not to feel bad if I couldn't make it out to dinner or whatever they asked me to do. I was not going to clutter up my mind with all of the extra things that go along with being a big leaguer."

That dedication and hard work paid off for Carpenter when

he won a reserve spot on the Cardinals as they broke camp in Florida and began the regular season. Still, Carpenter knew the 2012 season would be a challenging year for him. Ever since he had begun playing the game as a young boy, he had almost always been in the starting lineup. Learning how to handle playing only part of the time, and being relied on mainly as a pinch hitter, was a new experience for him.

But having a choice between being a bench player in the major leagues or starting every day in Triple-A is an easy choice for every player.

"As a bench player you are looking for those opportunities to come through and do your part and have an impact," Carpenter said. "Fortunately, I have been able to do that. Being a bench player and having to pinch-hit and come into games late is more mentally challenging than anything I've come across in this game.

"You are pretty much playing the game from the bench. Sitting there, you go through every situation because you don't know when or if you are going to get in there. You have to stay focused. If you are a pitcher or a regular just getting the day off, you can sometimes just hang out and do whatever. Playing off the bench you never know when your name is going to get called, and you always have to be ready."

Carpenter did a good job of that, coming through with eight hits in thirty-one pinch-hit at-bats, including five doubles, and driving in eleven runs. That total was tied for first among National League pinch hitters and was the highest total by a Cardinals rookie since Joe Frazier set the team record with fifteen RBI as a pinch hitter in 1954.

Carpenter's versatility also was important for the team, as he started games at first base, third base, left field, and right field, and even two games at second base. Along the way he enjoyed some very successful days, including going 4-for-4 with five RBI against the Cubs on April 15, and having another four-hit game on August 12 at Philadelphia. The fact that he had more than two hundred at-bats and played in more than half of the Cardinals' games came as a surprise to Carpenter.

"I figured and had it set in my mind that I was going to be a guy who might start every now and then," Carpenter said. "I've gone through some stretches due to teammates' injuries when I have been in the lineup quite a bit and had an opportunity to play. I'm grateful for being on the team and also for getting a chance to play as much as I have."

He's thankful to God for allowing that to happen, to make his childhood dreams come true. Everything he has gone through has not only made him more determined to succeed in the game, but has also made him more determined to succeed in life.

"I've always believed in the fact that strong Christians are strong people," he said. "You have your faith as a backbone. I believe what the Bible says about faith being the most important thing in your life, and that you should be fearless. There are a lot of things that can get in the way of performance like fear and worrying.

"That's where faith comes in and helps give you strength. You know a game is not the end-all. What happens in this game is all about having that mind-set, to know that in whatever you are doing you are doing it to the best of your ability. It tells us [that] in the Bible, and that's what drives me to be the player, husband, brother, and son that I am."

SIX

THE PROSPECTS: JAMES RAMSEY AND KOLTEN WONG

Then he said to them all: "Whoever wants to be my disciple must deny themselves and take up their cross daily and follow me."

—Luke 9:23 NIV

James Ramsey was in his apartment in Tallahassee, Florida, on the night of June 5, surrounded by family and friends, as the 2012 major league baseball draft came on the television.

Ramsey, the center fielder on Florida State's baseball team, had long dreamed of becoming a professional in the sport he loved, and one year earlier he had had a chance to make those dreams come true when he had been selected by the Minnesota Twins in the twenty-second round of the 2011 amateur draft. A junior at the time, Ramsey thought long and hard about whether to accept the Twins' offer, which eventually reached $500,000, an offer rivaling that of a second-round pick. He prayed about the decision and ultimately said no to the Twins in favor of returning to Florida State to complete his senior season.

"It was a little more than a baseball decision," Ramsey said. "I felt like I had some unfinished business at Florida State. I felt like I had a high platform for my faith and not just the city of Tallahassee but across all of college athletics. I was the president of two different campus organizations and had some leadership things to attend to for another year. I wanted to finish my degree and show people that you can go back and earn your degree that nobody can take from you."

As the 2012 draft began, however, Ramsey prayed that he had done the right thing and that another team would give him the opportunity to make those childhood dreams come true.

He had accomplished everything else he had wanted in the previous twelve months. He earned his finance degree, graduating magna cum laude with a 4.0 GPA. And, as the first team captain of the Seminoles during the thirty-three years Mark Martin had coached the team, Ramsey led the team to a berth in the College World Series in Omaha. He used the platform of his college positions to speak about his faith to as many people as he could reach, earning comparisons to another college athlete from Florida, quarterback Tim Tebow. And, while all of that was positive, one piece was yet unknown—whether he would be picked in the draft.

At the same time Ramsey was watching the television and waiting for news, Rob Fidler was in the Cardinals' war room doing the same thing. The team's area scout for Georgia and north Florida, Fidler was the person in the organization most familiar with Ramsey and his abilities. He saw him as a perfect fit for the Cardinals and was just hoping he would still be available when it came St. Louis's turn to draft.

"He was the one I was the most passionate about," Fidler said about the left-handed hitter. "I am supremely confident in what I saw in this kid. He was the guy I kept coming back to. He has off-the-charts makeup and phenomenal drive. People toss around the term *work ethic* a lot, but with this kid it's not just talk. He's a vocal guy, and his teammates love him."

Neither Ramsey nor Fidler had to wait long. After taking a pitcher, Michael Wacha from Texas A&M, as the nineteenth over-all choice, the Cardinals called Ramsey's name as the twenty-third overall selection in the draft.

"The whole year has been about Proverbs 19:21—a man can play his course, but the Lord determines his steps," Ramsey said. "I have really tried to trust upon that. For me, it wasn't necessarily result-oriented. It wasn't about becoming a first-rounder; it was to do the most with the platform that I have.

"The hard work I've put in, all the faith that I have kept in myself, the faith my teammates have kept in me—I wouldn't be in this position without God. I wouldn't be in this position without my teammates, my coaches, and my family. I did exactly what I came back to do."

Nobody was happier for Ramsey than Martin, the legendary coach at Florida State.

"He's a young man that St. Louis will really fall in love with," Martin said. "He's going to play hard every pitch and encourage those around him. St. Louis deserves James Ramsey and vice versa because I've been in that ballpark and I know how the fans treat everybody.

"Everybody who knows the guy understands his passion for the game. He doesn't accept anything but the best from himself and from those around him. He enjoys people. He's a man of God, he works as hard as any player I ever coached, and I've been blessed to have a number of outstanding players in my career. Nothing is easy in this game. He has a way of encouraging those who are struggling. He's a born leader and a young man who only comes along once in a while. He just happened to be a Seminole for the last four years.

"If anybody ever deserved to wear a C on his jersey it was

James Ramsey. More so than the way he plays the game, it's the way he conducts himself. This guy is one of a kind. How many Players of the Year, in the ACC or any outstanding baseball conference, will be the academic All-American of the Year? He had a 4.0 GPA this past semester and a 3.85 the first semester, in finance and accounting. He is a guy that really puts forth the effort in everything he does. He is president of the student athletic council that does so much here on campus, and he's working with Christian Ponder [Vikings quarterback and FSU alum] on another project. He's a special young man who truly cares about all people, but certainly his family is those on the baseball field and in the clubhouse with him.

"Rammer is not a guy that toots his own horn. He's a tough baseball player. He plays the game right. He is the way I would want my son to be. . . . He has run full speed into the wall so many times it's not funny. He's a gamer. He's going to go out every day and make St. Louis proud with the effort he puts forth."

As excited as he was, Ramsey was even more pleased to become a Cardinals prospect when he found out he could not have handpicked a better organization in which to continue his quest of combining his baseball talents with his strong faith.

"Immediately after the draft Cardinals fans and fans of FSU started telling me it was a perfect fit," Ramsey said, "especially after faith was one of the biggest reasons I decided to go back to school for my senior year. I definitely knew the Cardinals had a lot of great players, but I didn't know the depth of the strong believers on the team."

Ramsey became one of the two hundred–plus players in the Cardinals' minor league system when he signed his contract after Florida State was eliminated from the College World Series, and he was assigned to St. Louis's Class A affiliate in the Florida State League.

"To be the only player in this year's draft class sent straight to high A was the biggest compliment I could have received," Ramsey said. "The Cardinals wanted to challenge me and push me. You see great arms every day in this league, guys who are going to be in the big leagues in a couple of years."

After having a terrific senior year at Florida State, including being named the ACC Player of the Year and an All-American, the twenty-two-year-old Ramsey discovered that his performance on the field at Palm Beach did not match his previous success. For Ramsey, however, the summer was all about getting educated in the ways of professional baseball, learning how to prepare to play the game on a daily basis and deal with all of the frustrations and disappointments that are so intrinsic to the game.

Those people who viewed only his .229 batting average for the first fifty-six games of his professional career were missing the big picture, Ramsey said.

"The only thing I did not have success with was my batting average," Ramsey said. "I know that sounds a little strange because one of the ways people view success in baseball is through statistics. But I've had an opportunity to get better every day and establish relationships with my teammates and coaches. I'm very happy with my season. To view it only through statistics is a very short-sighted focus."

Ramsey, who grew up in a Christian home in the Atlanta suburb of Alpharetta, Georgia, also had the opportunity to grow and share his faith with a new audience—a change he had already experienced when he left high school for Florida State.

"I went from going to a private Christian school of about four hundred students, a small group of believers, to a school of more than forty thousand, where I was around a lot more nonbelievers," Ramsey said. "Nobody said it was going to be easy. When Jesus sent His disciples out, they didn't go where it was going to be easy.

But God is not going to put anything on your plate that you can't handle."

Dealing with a batting average one hundred points or so lower than what he had been used to was another challenge and adjustment for Ramsey, and he admits his faith helped him through what could have been considered a trying and disappointing season. He struck out four times in one game and three times in another.

"I am really confident every time I go to the plate that I will put together a tough at-bat," he said. "It's been fun. Pitchers know I was a first-round pick and they are going to try to get me out. I'm used to that. In college I know there always was a star next to my name on the scouting report.

"I always try to give God the glory in good times and bad times. God never turns His back on you. I can have a good day even if I go 0 for 5 because I was encouraging to a teammate or talked to somebody about Jesus.

"I want to make use of all of the talents God has given me. I also believe in working hard and putting in the effort to maximize those talents. It's all about striving to reach your potential."

One fact Ramsey soon learned about the Cardinals organization is that the team has fans everywhere. One of their more die-hard fans is Kyle Thompson, a native of Oklahoma who spent the entire 2012 season as a contestant in the MLB Fan Cave in New York. Ramsey met Thompson in the middle of September, getting a personalized tour of the Cave.

"It was like any other Sunday in the Cave when I heard a knock at the window," Thompson said. "Since we are in the middle of the Cave for all to see at all hours of the day, a knock was not surprising. However, I turned around to see Ramsey waving at me. He was visiting his brother who lives and works in New York, and wanted to stop by the Cave to 'visit the Cardinals fan.'

"We were able to find some time to sit in the downstairs lounge of the Fan Cave. I am not sure how it came up, but we quickly discovered that we were all Christians. In a city of ten million–plus people, you would not think that running into another Christian would be rare, but it was a rare occurrence for me. It was a breath of fresh air to sit with other Christians that also have a similar love of baseball.

"James and I have kept in touch via text messaging, phone calls, and Twitter since his visit to the Cave. We have even bounced concerns about our futures and how it relates to how God will use us down the road. He is definitely my brother in Christ."

In October, Ramsey was back in Florida, participating in the Cardinals' instructional league for about a month. After that came a trip to the Dominican Republic to work on an FCA-sponsored baseball camp at a school where his former high school coach is now serving a sabbatical. Preparations for the 2013 season began soon after that, and Ramsey is looking forward to growing as a baseball player and as a Christian.

Whenever he is asked for an autograph, Ramsey includes one of several of his favorite Bible verses, such as Luke 9:23.

"I've had people test me and ask me what the verse says," Ramsey said. "I've always been able to tell them."

Ramsey soon learned that one of the many players in the organization who shared his beliefs about baseball and about God was second baseman Kolten Wong, the Cardinals' first-round pick out of Hawaii in 2011.

In all your ways acknowledge Him,
And He will make your paths straight.

—Proverbs 3:6 NASB

Kolten Wong's faith is with him every day—his favorite Bible verse, Proverbs 3:6, is tattooed onto his back.

"I got it done last winter, when I was back home in Hawaii," Wong said. "It was a verse I always had stuck in my head. It was pretty painful, but it was worth it."

Wong spent the 2012 season playing second base for the Cardinals' Double-A farm team in Springfield, Missouri. The organization's first-round pick in the 2011 draft out of the University of Hawaii has quickly progressed from playing college baseball to being one of the top prospects in the St. Louis organization.

In his first full season in professional baseball, twenty-one-year-old Wong became an All-Star and was selected to play in the Futures Game as part of the All-Star game festivities in Kansas City. Later in the year he earned an invitation to play in the Arizona Fall League, loaded with the best prospects from the minor leagues. Wong, praised by the Cardinals for his work ethic and the way he goes about his job, knows who to credit for his success.

"In baseball, no matter what you do, you have to give all the praise and glory to God," he said. "If you do that, He will always have your back and will always be with you. I've constantly seen things happen because I have done that."

Even though he has been in the minor leagues for only a short period of time, Wong knows it is where he needs to grow and mature if he is going to advance to the major leagues. He sees the same fact as being true about his growth as a follower of Christ.

It was something the Springfield hitting coach, Phil Wellman, said to him one day in the middle of the season that brought that point home on a personal level.

"Before, I had always given praise to God when I got a hit, but when I didn't get a hit, I would go back to the dugout all ticked off," Wong said. "Phil just said to me one day, 'I know you are a follower of Christ. The thing you need to do is always give Him the praise and glory.' I sat back and thought about it, and realized that that made a lot of sense.

"Ever since then I have tried to do that. I pray before the game and thank Him for how I am going to play, and I pray afterward and thank Him for being safe and having a good game, whether it was bad or good. Just being able to play makes it a good day."

Wong has had more good days than bad since he began playing baseball as a youngster in Hawaii, the son of a former minor league player. He was a catcher in high school before switching to second base in college. He went to the prestigious Cape Cod League after his sophomore season and was named the league's MVP, which put him on the radar for professional teams selecting players in the 2011 draft.

After being picked as the twenty-second overall choice in the 2011 draft, Wong quickly agreed to a contract and joined the Class A Quad Cities River Bandits, where he hit .335 in forty-seven games and helped the team win the Midwest League championship.

Wong, like teammate Oscar Taveras, made the jump from low Class A to Double-A at the start of the 2012 season, skipping an entire level because the Cardinals thought he was ready and could handle the challenge. Wong was grateful for the opportunity.

"It's been a real big learning experience for me," he said. "I've seen a lot of things I can work on, and there are a lot of things I have gotten better at. One thing everybody talks about is the grind of learning how to get through the long season. I've learned how to take care of my body—what to do and what not to do. There are just little things that can help a lot."

Wong has experienced what life in the minor leagues is supposed to be about—the learning that can come from twelve-hour bus rides, the growth that can come from an 0-for-6 night. He had already played the game long enough as an amateur to realize baseball is more a game of failure than success, but he had that lesson reinforced to him many times during the Springfield season.

"You know you are going to fail so many times," he said. "All the times you want to yell out and say to God, 'What's going on? Why aren't You helping me?' is when you just have to keep the faith."

For the season, the five-foot-nine Wong posted a .287 average with 9 home runs, 52 RBI, and 21 stolen bases. He helped lead the team to the North Division title in the second half of the regular season, then earn a berth in the championship series against Frisco, the Double-A farm team of the Texas Rangers. Wong ended his season as a champion for the second consecutive time, as Springfield defeated Frisco to win the 2012 Texas League title.

Wong's education in faith has been as important to him as his baseball education.

"I think I'm growing a lot more," he said. "I grew up kind of knowing about God, but not really that much on a personal level. As I started getting older, I got closer to God, taking it more seriously and starting to go to church every Sunday and read the Bible. I have had a lot of experiences where I've seen how God can work in our lives, and that has showed me how strong He is. Before, I was really quiet about my faith."

Wong started to realize that it was okay to be more open about his faith when he saw some of the major league Cardinals and how they acted. Outfielder Matt Holliday made certain Wong was one of several players he brought to St. Louis for a long weekend in the winter, trying to acclimate them a little to the city, Busch Stadium, and some of their future teammates. Then, as a nonroster invitee to spring training, Wong also was able to watch Holliday, David Freese, and others as they participated in the team's weekly Bible study and chapel sessions.

"We didn't really talk much about faith," said Wong, who didn't need words to watch the power of faith in how Holliday,

Freese, and the others went about their work and their daily lives. "We started talking more at spring training, and that's when I started to realize how deep [Holliday] was into religion."

It also was during spring training when Wong began to take his own faith to another level. Former Cardinal Zack Cox challenged his minor league teammates each week by giving them a new Bible verse that they had to try to memorize by the end of the week.

"I tried to do that, but I also wanted to read it so I could more than just memorize it, and try to comprehend it to my own understanding. That's worked really well," Wong said. "I keep my Bible on the nightstand next to my bed, and I try to read every night before I go to sleep. It's kind of like my night reading, going through and finding a few verses."

Wong is no different than every minor leaguer in one respect: he prays that some day he will find himself playing in the major leagues. That could happen as soon as the 2013 season.

"You have to realize God has a plan for everyone," he said. "I strongly believe that. I've had a lot of times where I've sat back and went, 'Wow, when am I going to get a break?' I just keep telling myself to keep the faith, to believe in God, and He's helped me out a lot."

SEVEN

RICK HORTON

Trust in the LORD with all thine heart; and lean not unto thine own
understanding.
In all thy ways acknowledge him, and he shall direct thy paths.

—Proverbs 3:5–6 KJV

Former Cardinals pitcher Rick Horton was in Kansas City on
June 22, 2012, preparing for the Fox Sports Midwest telecast of
the opening game of the team's three-game series against the
Royals. In spirit, however, Horton was far away; his mind kept
drifting back to another June 22, ten years earlier. That day in
2002 remains one of the saddest in Horton's life and one of the
most somber days in the history of the Cardinals.

At the time, Horton was working part-time on Cardinals'
radio broadcasts, filling in whenever someone was on vacation or
away on another assignment. He was not with the Cardinals in
Chicago on that day as the team prepared for a nationally televised
game against the Cubs at Wrigley Field. Horton, who since 1993
has also worked as the executive director of the St. Louis chapter
of the Fellowship of Christian Athletes, was at home watching
television shortly before the game was scheduled to begin.

"I saw a crawl on the screen which said a Cardinals pitcher had died, but I missed the first part of the crawl, and I didn't know who it was," Horton said. "Even before I found out, I went to my bedroom and starting packing. The only thought I had was *I've got to get to Chicago.*

"It was odd. I just had a sense, and I really wasn't sure why I was going. My mind just thought it was the right thing to do."

While he was packing, Horton saw on the television that it was Darryl Kile, a thirty-three-year-old pitcher, who had died. He still did not know any circumstances beyond that basic fact.

His telephone rang, and calling from Wrigley Field was Mark O'Neill, the team's assistant trainer. He was calling on behalf of general manager Walt Jocketty, both to tell Horton what had happened and also to ask if Horton and Walt Enoch, who also works with the FCA chapter and the chapel services for the Cardinals, could accompany some front-office personnel to Chicago.

An hour or so later, the group assembled at the airport and flew to Chicago on a private jet belonging to one of the teams owners.

Horton had no idea what he was going to do, but he knew he needed to be there to offer whatever assistance he could. In addition to his broadcasting duties, he wore another hat with the team because of his faith and his work with the FCA: helping out with the team's chapel services and Bible studies. The Cardinals players, coaches, and manager Tony La Russa were back at their downtown hotel by the time the group got there, and Horton joined his friends who were trying to come to grips with what had happened.

By that time, Horton had learned that Kile had never arrived at Wrigley Field that morning. Calls to his cell phone and hotel room went unanswered. Finally, hotel security and Cardinals officials entered Kile's room and found him dead in bed. Tests later revealed Kile had died in his sleep from a heart attack.

The loss came only four days after the death of legendary broadcaster Jack Buck, who had worked for the Cardinals for close to fifty years. While Buck had been in ill health for some time, his death still had hit the organization, its fans, and the entire city of St. Louis hard. Now, suddenly, came the unexpected death of a player in the prime of his life.

"It was one of the hardest things I've ever had to deal with," Horton said. "I had to see people in pain and hurting. Players like Dave Veres and Mike Matheny . . . I can still picture their faces and that of Edgar Rentería. The pain of that was just awful to be around. I wanted to help guys, but I couldn't fix the problem.

"I was grateful that we had a couple of gentlemen there who were professionals in dealing with grief situations. They said to me, 'Look, you have the relationships with these guys. We will help you help them.'"

The game that day was canceled, but the decision was made to play on Sunday night in another nationally televised game. For the first time in his life, Matheny, who had been extremely close to Kile, refused to play, arguing for the postponement of that game too. His grief was just too great.

The two had been inseparable. Kile had once told La Russa that if Matheny was not catching him, then Kile wasn't pitching. Another time, Kile, on the occasion of winning his twentieth game in 2000, had presented Matheny with a Rolex watch as a thank-you gift, knowing Matheny's affinity for wearing cheap knockoff watches. As Matheny sat in the trainer's room at Wrigley hours after learning of Kile's death, he pulled out the stem, stopping the watch and freezing the moment in time. He has never reinserted the stem, and he says he never will.

"One of the things that was so tough was that, in the baseball world, you are taught to grind every day," Horton said. "There is always another game and then another game. You see other people smiling and laughing at the ballpark and wanting to be entertained. The show must go on. But these guys were dealing with such personal grief and angst and what they were going through was just so tough.

"Baseball people tend to think they are invincible. We all think that we are going to continue and not get hurt and play forever. You don't want to entertain the negatives of possibly getting hurt or worse. That made it just a really confusing time in a lot of ways and a real test for all of the players."

Jocketty asked Horton to help enlist the help of other former players and strong Christians, such as Todd Worrell and Kent Bottenfield, to ask if they could be at the ballpark as much as possible to create an additional support network. It was not just the players and the former teammates who were suffering, but the other clubhouse and team personnel who had known and been close to Kile.

For Horton, this was a personal test as well. As a broadcaster, he had one set of responsibilities. As the director of the FCA chapter who helped lead the team's chapel and Bible studies, he wore another hat. The possibility of a conflict between the two forced him at times to pull back and not be as involved as he would have liked.

"I didn't want it to get to the point where players on the team who were not Christians or not involved in going to chapel or Bible study thought I was treating them differently because I didn't have the same kind of relationship with them," Horton said. "You also run that risk in the media of dividing people because of your beliefs. I want to have everybody united.

"If I am in a room having chapel with sixteen guys, then I don't want the guys who are not there thinking I am giving preferential treatment to them. I've always faced that battle. I pulled back somewhat because I did not want to compromise the Christian guys on the team, or alienate any of the other guys."

Horton has seen examples of that in the past, including during the year he spent as a minor league pitching coach in the Indians' farm system after the end of his playing career.

"I had a pitcher come up to me one day and say, 'I know the Christian guys know something that I don't know and I want you to tell me what it is,'" Horton said. "It was after practice, so I brought him into my office and told him."

The player became a Christian and went on to pitch in the major leagues and became a husband and father. He still exchanges Christmas cards with Horton every year.

"That made that whole summer of coaching worthwhile for me," Horton said.

While Horton was able to provide that one player with an answer, one of the hardest truths of dealing with Kile's death was the reality that there were no obvious or understandable answers about why God had taken him that day.

"One of the great principles which I tried to share was that we don't always have to have answers," Horton said. "Sometimes there aren't any discernible to us at this time in our [lives] and to our understanding. That's where faith kicks in. It's not that God caused that situation to happen—what faith tells you is that He cares about all of us and that provides comfort and peace from an eternal perspective."

Horton was one of those who watched the Cardinals regroup and dedicate the rest of their season "to Darryl," whose uniform number was 57. Amazingly, the team went on to win fifty-seven more games that season after Kile's death, as they won the National League Central and qualified for the postseason.

Now, ten years later, as Horton prepared for another game and another broadcast, that fact is still hard for him to comprehend.

"I've had very melancholy moments about [Kile] and Jack Buck," Horton said. "It's difficult for me to separate the two.

They were very different situations, and I knew Jack so much better. He was the guy who told me I should go into broadcasting. I am indebted to him for his friendship and support. I am frustrated that we did not make a bigger deal of it, but I realize there are young players here who don't know who Darryl Kile was. The reality is that things change. If you don't know, you don't remember."

Nobody has to tell Horton how much things change. He is a living example, because there was a point in his life when Horton would not have considered himself a Christian. After growing up in a Christian home in Hyde Park, New York, going to church every Sunday, Horton went off to college at the University of Virginia, where he played baseball while majoring in engineering. It was there that he turned his back on religion.

"That was a time in my life when I would have at least considered myself an agnostic if not an atheist," Horton said. "I was very anti-religion and very anti-spirituality. I saw spirituality as a weakness. I kind of saw it as a way not to face life or responsibilities, to put off problems and potential solutions.

"The education and training I received there was phenomenal, but really college was a dark time in my life in a lot of ways, especially spiritually. I thought I had the world by the tail and I could do whatever I wanted. My critical bend and my cutting humor kind of defined me in college."

The Cardinals selected the left-handed Horton in the fourth round of the 1980 amateur draft and assigned him to their Class A farm team in St. Petersburg, Florida. He had the same feelings then about religion and faith as he had had in college, and it would be a couple of years before that changed.

Then, at the age of twenty-two, while playing Double-A baseball in Little Rock, Arkansas, a teammate gave Horton a Bible.

"There were some very solid Christian athletes on that

team, and I saw a difference in them," Horton said. "I had team-mates who represented what it meant to be a Christian man in different ways."

Horton started reading the Bible and, for the first time, started to believe it was the Word of God. The more he read, the stronger his belief grew.

"Things were slowly being revealed to me," Horton said. "I had a love for reading God's Word, and it spoke to me."

One of the first realities that became apparent to Horton was his level of sin.

"I think the gospel starts with the self-recognition of our imper-fections and our sin," he said. "I became a better friend, I became more patient, and I didn't have the same levels of harshness. Reading the Bible brought me peace and joy. It was right around that time that I was dating Ann [his future wife], and part of my joy was being able to share the gospel with her."

While Horton found strength in the Bible, he also saw it in some of his teammates, and in one teammate in particular. Larry Reynolds was an outfielder on the team, a product of Stanford University who was a couple of years older than Horton. He also was a very strong Christian.

"He was probably the most influential teammate I had," Horton said. "He was kind of our chapel leader. He also had played football at Stanford and I just saw a tremendous faith in the way he played the game, and the way he dealt with people. He also was extremely bright.

"I had a stumbling block in that I thought faith was a sign of weakness or ignorance, and here was a guy with a brain embrac-ing the truth of the gospel. I had never really put those two things together. He represented a big turning point for me."

Horton also became good friends that year with another future major leaguer and strong Christian, Andy Van Slyke, and now looks back fondly on that season as the start of his religious journey, which is still going strong thirty years later.

"There is something about reading the Word and having it speak to me that prompted the big change in my life," Horton said. "It takes time. There are times now that I'm older that you still learn things. You think you know everything, and then you find out you don't know half of what you thought you knew. That's true in spiritual understanding too."

It was less than two years later that Horton made his debut in the major leagues, another moment he will never forget. He gave up a home run to the first batter he faced, Jeffrey Leonard of the San Francisco Giants, which taught him the immediate lesson that pitching in the major leagues was not going to be easy, just as being a Christian isn't easy either.

One of Horton's favorite parts of the Bible is the book of John. He read a commentary about that book and found an analogy that he thought applied to the rest of the Bible as well.

"It's shallow enough for you to wade in and it's deep enough for an elephant to swim in," Horton said. "I think that's a great description not only of the book of John but also of the Bible in general and to faith in general. You can swim in the shallows, or wade in the shallows of faith and enjoy the fellowship and connection with other believers and family. But there is a time when you have to swim out in deeper waters and tangle with deeper issues. You have to be careful not to spend too much time out there or you might drown."

The more Horton understands the simplicity, and the depth, of the Bible and faith, the more he can draw a connection between that and baseball.

"When I was coaching, I found myself walking out to the mound and telling the pitchers the same thing I would later tell twelve-year-old kids when I was coaching my son's team," Horton said. "Maybe you communicate it with slightly different language, but it was still the basics about the game, about throwing strikes, getting ahead in the count, about hitters driving through the ball, about discipline and good balance. There's a thirty-year-old professional version of that and a twelve-year-old version, but there's such a gap about what it means and how to get there.

"As you mature, that's the fun of the pursuit. I had a college humanities professor who said one time, and it remains one of my favorite quotes, that if you really understand something, you can explain it clearly to a PhD and to a kindergartner. There's simplicity to it, but there's also a depth to it. Baseball is that way, and I think faith is that way."

As he has continued to live the dual life of baseball and faith in his two jobs, broadcasting and being an FCA leader, Horton has become more confident that he can coexist in both worlds and not shortchange either of his employers—or God.

It is easier to connect the two with the 2012 version of the Cardinals, Horton said, because of the strong Christian leadership on the team and in the manager's office.

"When you have prominent players such as Wainwright and Berkman saying that chapel is a good thing for us, it becomes undisputable in the clubhouse," Horton said. "That's kind of the way it is with leadership and the veterans' presence. One thing the veterans on this team do really well is realize this is still a team, and that they may believe differently than their teammates, but we still have to love our teammates. They are not in a theological battle every day with their teammates."

Horton believes that the ability to coexist with a teammate, even if he does not agree with his religious beliefs, comes with maturity. He also knows that everybody has to decide for themselves what is best for them, what they want to believe. Nobody on the Cardinals, Horton said, tries to push religion on somebody else. It is there if the player wants it, but if not, nobody is going to get upset or think less of him because of his decision.

"I think a mature Christian realizes such a nonconnection between faith and the game," Horton said. "I can remember a time when I was not a Christian and I thought that was what they were doing. I thought the Christians were having that little good-luck charm, a mumbo jumbo thing."

After he accepted Christ into his life, Horton realized that was not the case.

"I think God is concerned about our hearts," Horton said. "Performance is not the bottom line. He cares about our hearts seeking Him, period. It doesn't have to do with how many hits you get, but yet I know there are people who think that way. One of my favorite questions now that I like to ask is, 'What is it that you think I believe?' The answers I get to that question are crazy.

"You don't have to read very far in the Bible to see the struggles and pain and failures of God's people when they are carrying out His work. It's not like some big Harlequin story where everything ends with some great wonderful storyline. It's just not like that. A lot of people think that's what [Christians] think."

Horton knows he was not the first non-Christian to think of Christians as weak, and that they were using religion as a crutch, especially when it came to athletics. He has also seen many examples of a player striking out in the ninth inning to end a game and having the player say it was "God's will." He doesn't believe either of those feelings to be true.

"It's an age-old battle that people have fought throughout time, that faith will make you soft," Horton said. "I find it to be very unbiblical, even though it may be true in certain cases. You are not going to say that about Adam Wainwright. Are you going to say he doesn't play hard? He's a bulldog between the lines, but he can be funny and goofy and spiritual off the field. He goes onto the field to beat you. Other guys on this team are the same way.

"The other thing I like about this team is nobody has a sense that if they say something about their faith they will get slammed. You don't see a guy getting downgraded because he wants to read the Bible. There probably was a time in this game where that was true, although not necessarily in St. Louis. Some teams have chapel and Bible study and tolerate it, and some teams have it and support it. I would say the Cardinals are in the latter category."

At the same time, however, Horton and the other chapel leaders realize and understand that baseball activities have to be the priority of the team. They will never schedule chapel or Bible study when players should be on the field for batting practice, and they have tried to determine what the proper amount of time is to devote to their religious meetings.

"Of all of the teams I played on, I don't know if I was on a team that had more guys interested in coming to chapel and professing their faith," said Worrell. "It's kind of a business thing which has crept into the church . . . that we tend to quantify success by numbers. But we would be doing what we were doing if we only had one guy there. It's kind of like the parable of the lost sheep."

The focus of the team's Bible study for much of the 2012 season was the book of Galatians.

"It changes in different years," said Worrell, the president of the St. Louis FCA chapter, "but it's about the redemption of man, how important the cross is, the sacrifice that Jesus made. That's really what the whole Bible is about, about the redemption of man and what God has prepared for man beyond this life, the glory of His kingdom to come. I don't care what book of the Bible you are in; it comes back to the cross.

"That's what the message needs to be and where we need to

be sharing it. That's where God has the biggest impact on touching people's lives."

Worrell said that another topic that frequently comes up is how God uses the lives of His followers to reach other people, and how what an athlete does off the field is just as important as what he does on the field when it comes to leading a Christian lifestyle.

"A lot of athletes out there think that God is helping them throw the pitch or hit a home run, like there is a physical pull or magical touch, and I don't believe that," Worrell said. "I believe God's priority for each individual is to have a relationship with Him and that what happens on the baseball field is the athlete's responsibility. He gives them the talent and ability; they are responsible for honing it.

"I don't think God's will has anything to do with an athlete's performance. It's so human to have a theology like that, like God is choosing which believer on a particular day He is going to choose to win. God doesn't operate like that."

That is a philosophy the Cardinals understand and accept. Horton believes one of the most important tenets of a person's faith has to be that there will be times, such as when Darryl Kile died for no apparent reason, that there just is no earthly explanation for why something happened.

"My favorite Bible verse is Proverbs 3:5–6, because it reminds me that I am not as smart as I think I am," Horton said. "My initial step of faith is to realize my own ignorance. It's a reminder for me that just when I think I have it figured out, something else is going to happen."

EIGHT

BARRET BROWNING

I trust in you;
do not let me be put to shame,
nor let my enemies triumph over me.

—Psalm 25:2 NIV

Barret Browning was on the bus, setting up his bed for the over-night ride from Memphis to Oklahoma City, after the Redbirds' game on June 29. A veteran of six years in the minor leagues, Browning had a lot of experience riding buses.

While Browning was trying to ensure his comfort for the seven-hour ride, he had no idea that his manager, Pop Warner, was on the telephone, talking with the Cardinals' general manager, John Mozeliak. That night the Cardinals had lost 14–5 to the Pirates, going through most of their bullpen, and were in need of some fresh arms for their game the next afternoon.

It was decided that Memphis would send Browning, a twenty-seven-year-old left-handed reliever who had been pitching well for the Triple-A team, and Maikel Cleto, a right-handed reliever, to St. Louis. Relievers Eduardo Sanchez and Sam Freeman would be making the trip in the opposite direction.

Warner sent word out to the team bus that he needed to talk to Browning.

"A guy who works for the Redbirds came on the bus, and I heard somebody calling my name," Browning said. "I looked up, and he was waving for me to get off the bus. I didn't really think too much about it. I took another couple of minutes to finish getting my bed ready, then went to see what he wanted. He said, 'Pop wants to talk to you.'"

Usually, when a manager wants to talk to a player in the minor leagues in such a manner, it means something has happened that will affect his status—either moving up or down a level. Browning had just been named to the Triple-A All-Star team, so his immediate reaction was that maybe, just maybe, he was finally getting the call from the major leagues.

"We had a good relationship, but he had never called me into his office except to tell me I had made the Triple-A All-Star team," Browning said. "I knew something was up. It was not a very far walk from the bus to his office, but the whole time I kept saying to myself, 'God, please let this be it, please let this be it.'

"I was saying it out loud, almost like a prayer. I thought it was a possibility, and I know I was kind of speed walking to get to his office."

When he got there, Warner and pitching coach Blaise Ilsley were waiting for him.

"The first thing he said to me was, 'I just want to let you know the All-Star thing is not going to work out,'" Browning said. "I said, 'Really? Okay.' Then he said, 'Because you are going to the big leagues.'

"I lost all feeling in my body. It was amazing. I just thought about all of the hard work I had put in. I know it probably was not much different than when anybody else is told that news, but there were a million emotions going through my head.

"I got a little teary-eyed while I was talking to them. I had played against Pop's teams for three years in Double-A and he knew my road, the struggles, the highs and the lows. I think they wanted it for me as much as I wanted it. That has got to be the best part of a minor league manager's job."

After leaving the manager's office, Browning couldn't think of what he needed to do first. He had to call his wife, Meah. He had to call his parents back in Georgia. He had to go back to his apartment and pack. Because the Cardinals were playing a day game the following day, there were no flights available that could get him and Cleto to St. Louis in time for the game, so one of the Memphis front-office employees agreed to drive them, leaving in about six hours.

Browning first called his wife. He had to repeat the news about six or seven times before she finally believed him. Then came the phone call to his parents, waking them up in the early-morning hours, a phone call they didn't mind getting. Despite Browning telling them he would pay for them and his brother to fly to St. Louis the next day, they hopped in the car and began the thirteen-hour drive.

Browning's wife did fly to St. Louis, and all of the family arrived at Busch Stadium in time to see him take the mound in the sixth inning and retire all six batters he faced in his major league debut. It was, Browning said, literally a dream come true, a dream he often believed might go unfulfilled.

Browning had been pitching in the minor leagues since 2006, signing with the Angels after being drafted in the twenty-eighth round. It was the fourth time he had been selected in the baseball draft—he had been previously drafted once out of high school, once out of junior college, and again after his junior year at Florida State. Each of the previous times he did not believe it was the right decision for him to sign.

"I had just turned seventeen when I was a senior in high

school," Browning said. "I was a grade ahead of where I should have been, and I knew there was physical room to grow and maturity to gain. Part of the decision each time was money, but it really was the least of my worries. I just sat down with my parents and the people I respected and loved, and got their opinions. The common consensus was that education can't be taken away, and if something happens in baseball, you still have an education and can provide for a wife and family."

Browning thought more about that as the 2012 season began. It was his first year with the Cardinals, who picked him up in the minor league portion of the Rule 5 draft. While he was grateful for the fresh start, he still had begun the season contemplating the end of his playing career.

"If I had spent all of this year at Triple-A, I was probably going to go home when the year was over," Browning said. "It was a decision I was going to continue praying about, but as far as I was concerned, that was going to be it."

Browning wasn't certain what he would do other than finish his degree, and then check what options were available to him. Those future plans, however, got put on hold when the call came to join the Cardinals.

One of the biggest reasons in Browning's mind for his promotion was a renewed emphasis he had made to put his faith in God to determine the future and course of his career.

"No doubt faith played a key role," Browning said. "Something definitely changed. I feel like we make our biggest strides as Christians and as believers when we are at our lowest points. It's easy when things are going great, when you are getting all the things you want in your life, the things you prayed for and dreamed of. When things are going good it's easy to say, 'Alright God, I got this right now. When I need You, I will call You.' That's something almost every Christian struggles with.

"The past six years have been hard for me. I went into this season really thinking this was going to be my last year. I was going to go out and have a good time and trust in Him that whatever happens is what He wants to happen, and where He wants me to be, that's where I'm going to be. If they send me home, I am supposed to be home. That's what He's got in mind for me.

"I just kind of relaxed and trusted my ability that He gave me and continued to work hard to groom that ability. I'm a firm believer that if you don't show that blessing ample respect and give it the nurturing it needs to improve, then He will take it away from you or won't use it in that way."

It was over the winter, while pitching in the Dominican Republic, that Browning decided he needed to do a better job of putting his faith in God. He knew he was leaving the Los Angeles Angels organization and welcomed the new beginning with the Cardinals, and he wanted to go into spring training with an improved attitude and desire. One of the people who helped him with that adjustment was Oakland outfielder Brandon Moss, one of his winter league teammates.

"There were a couple of really good Christian guys on the team, including Brandon," Browning said. "We read books and passed them around, and really discussed the Word. It helped me to realize those guys had been through a lot as well. Through Brandon I just learned to go out and play the game and love it. You have to appreciate every day you have and allow God to make the moves, whether it's what you want or not. I was really happy for him and what he did in Oakland, because he's a living example of what he was teaching me.

"You can get hurt two ways in this game—by not working hard enough and by trying to do too much. I just saw the value in relaxing and letting my ability come to be. You have to trust that God will keep you at your best. There is no doubt that is my situation."

Even though Browning would have liked to have had a longer stay in the majors before he was sent back down to Memphis, that first day of pitching at Busch Stadium against the Pirates made all of his struggles worthwhile.

With his parents and wife in the stands, Browning could have been nervous, but his teammates and the support personnel in the clubhouse made him feel as if he had been a major leaguer for years.

"I can't think of many guys I didn't talk to that first day," said Browning, including his former college teammate at Florida State, Shane Robinson. "Everyone was genuine in their appreciation for my contributions, and my happiness at being here."

That didn't really surprise Browning, because he had seen examples of that during spring training and also while pitching in Memphis.

"An organization doesn't have the history and tradition this organization has without good people who have good character," Browning said. "That includes the front office, the minor league office, the coaching staff, the training staff, even the people who work in the kitchen. They have good people doing their job with a good attitude and a smile on their face. Everybody is pulling on the same end of the rope. You could see it. I knew it in minor league camp.

"I sat and watched the way they went about their business. There was an expectation that everybody was going to do their job and be a professional and a good teammate. I was kind of nervous and wanted to fit in."

That became easier the first night Browning attended the team's weekly family Bible study.

"I had heard about it, but I didn't go the first week because my wife was there with me and I had not seen her much while I was in the Dominican over the winter," Browning said. "The next week

I went and I was blown away. There were eighty or ninety people there, including wives and kids. They had childcare set up and provided food. It was a real relaxed environment."

One of the aspects of the group's discussions, which surprised Browning, was how open the Cardinals players were about the importance of faith in their lives and their love of God.

"There was nobody there trying to protect his image from one another," Browning said. "We all live the same lifestyle, we have the same temptations and same stresses and responsibilities. They were very open the way they spoke about their personal lives and told things I have never heard other people willing to admit, things I have never been willing to admit. It was a great feeling that you could relax with these guys and talk with them and that they were not going to judge you, on or off the field. They were going to pull with you and build you up.

"They wanted to teach you, and not just be there. They were like a family. You hear a lot of players say that about their teammates, but it really is because it has to be. We really do pull for one another."

Seeing that in action during the season only increased Browning's appreciation for his new teammates, one of the primary reasons why he was disappointed when he was returned to Memphis in the middle of August.

"My faith grew every day, and that's how I knew I was in a good place," Browning said. "It's an old adage, but it's true that if you are not going forward you are either standing still or going backwards. My hope is that I can draw closer to the Lord every single day. There are days when I feel like I took a step back or didn't do anything to make that happen.

"But there are so many Christian guys here living a Christian lifestyle and everybody understands that we are humans and are going to make mistakes. It's encouraging to see so many guys doing that and to realize you are not alone trying to do it by yourself. I know the Lord is here for me, but at the same time I've got brothers in here with me, standing side by side."

There were times, Browning admits, during his minor league years when he did feel alone, and when his faith was tested in multiple ways. The most frequent question he asked God in those years was, why?

"At whatever league I was in, anytime I was pitching well and somebody else got the call to go up, it was discouraging and frustrating," Browning said. "The first thing you want to do is ask God why. If I had a dollar for every time I asked why, I would have made a lot more money than I'll ever make playing this game.

"This is a sport based on human error, which is why I love baseball more than any of the other sports. This sport is based on doing things consistently. No other sport has an 'E' column on the scoreboard. It can be very frustrating. It doesn't matter if I make a small mistake or an infielder misses a ground ball or an outfielder misses a fly ball. There are going to be errors. It's overcoming them that's important.

"This game has taught me that and helped me with my faith. There are times when things are not your fault but you could have done better. That's similar to life when things are not your fault, and that you have no control over, but you have to persevere and trust in God that He is going to pull you through."

The start to Browning's major league career could not have gone better. He retired the first thirteen batters he faced, spread across four games, before finally giving up a hit. In twelve games during the month of July, Browning faced thirty-three batters and gave up only five hits and three walks, holding opponents to a .167 batting average.

The lows that are bound to come after the highs in the game, however, found Browning in two games in Philadelphia, August

10 and 12, when he suffered the first two losses of his career. He gave up a two-run homer to Chase Utley in the eighth inning in a 1–1 game, and two days later, after pitching a scoreless tenth inning, gave up an RBI infield single with two outs to Juan Pierre in the Phillies' walk-off win.

Browning did not pitch again until August 18, when he picked up the first win of his major league career against the Pittsburgh Pirates, but the highs and lows of a relief pitcher caught up with him again the next afternoon, when he was the losing pitcher in a nineteen-inning game against the Pirates.

"Everybody on this team fought to win this game," a dejected Browning said in a quiet locker room after the nearly six-hour game. "Everybody did their job except me. I don't think I've ever been this disappointed. It doesn't get much worse.

"I was ready to pitch. I just didn't get the job done."

A home run by Pedro Alvarez off a 1–2 slider that caught too much of the plate ignited a three-run inning which carried the Pirates to the victory.

Browning said he had once pitched in a game that was longer— a twenty-six-inning game while he was in college at Florida State. "Took home the win," he said. "I wish this had happened the same way."

Browning knew the way he would get over the disappointment of that game, however, was the same way he had always gotten through the toughest moments in his life—through his faith in God.

Even when he received the disappointing news a few days later that he was being sent back to Memphis, Browning tried to keep a positive attitude. He knew that he had shown, to the Cardinals and other teams, that he could be a left-handed specialist, brought into games specifically to face left-handed batters. The times he got into trouble in his twenty-two games in the majors usually were when he was asked to pitch in different situations.

Left-handed batters had only a .194 average against Browning in those games, going 7–of–36, with five of the seven hits singles. He also retired nineteen of the first twenty-two batters he faced, an important statistic for a relief pitcher.

He pitched in five more games for Memphis before the end of their season, working 36 2/3 scoreless innings, but was not recalled to the majors when the rosters expanded. Instead he went home to Georgia, thinking about his future and hoping that one month in St. Louis would not turn out to be the total of his major league career.

"I think I had success against lefties, which is what I was expected to do," Browning said. "When I was asked to do more than that, I expect myself to do the job. I don't know what the Cardinals' plans are for me, but I know left-handers who can get left-handed batters out can have a job for a long time, and I hope that's the case."

Browning said, if anything, his month of being in the major leagues only increased his desire to work harder to get back to that level and stay there.

"I'm definitely going to continue playing," he said. "A lot of people say getting to the big leagues is the easy part, and staying there is the hard part, but I know it's hard to get there too. I worked too hard to get there and have that be it."

NINE

KYLE MCCLELLAN

What, then, shall we say in response to these things? If God is for us, who can be against us?

—**Romans 8:31** NIV

As the Cardinals gathered at Busch Stadium for a workout on July 12, the final day of the 2012 All-Star break, Matt Holliday looked across the locker room and noticed pitcher Kyle McClellan wearing a sling on his right arm.

McClellan had been out of action for almost two months because of an elbow injury, but he had begun throwing and was believed close to rejoining the Cardinals for the second half of the season. Instead, while rehabbing his elbow, McClellan discovered that he needed surgery on his shoulder to correct an injury he had been trying to pitch through for more than a year.

"Nobody rehabs their elbow and shows up having shoulder surgery," Holliday said.

Well, McClellan did. Two days earlier he had undergone the operation to repair frayed cartilage and a capsule problem. The surgery meant that McClellan's 2012 season was over after he had pitched in only sixteen games.

The doctors found that he had hurt his elbow because of the shoulder problem, which prevented McClellan from raising his elbow above his shoulder. This limitation caused him to pitch at an odd angle, which eventually hurt his elbow. The injury really was nothing new for McClellan, who had undergone Tommy John surgery while in the minors and has had to fight through other injuries during his career. He overcame the 2005 operation to make it to the majors three years later. At the time of the surgery, McClellan didn't know if he would ever get that chance to fulfill a childhood dream. That was when he realized he needed to develop a stronger faith in God.

"Looking back on it, it was the best thing that ever happened in my life," McClellan said. "I was twenty-one years old, I was immature, and I thought I was going to play baseball the rest of my life. To have the possibility that it might be taken away from me definitely changed my perspective."

McClellan had met his future wife by then, and with a wedding planned for the near future, he knew it also was time to get Christ more involved in his life.

"I grew up in the church but I never really grabbed hold of it and started to learn more about it until I got engaged," he said. "I knew I was going to start a family, and this was something I wanted to have for a base."

Luckily for McClellan, the St. Louis native was able to overcome that operation and continue his career. When he made it to the Cardinals, he became one of a select few players who ever got the chance to play for their hometown team.

He had signed with the organization after being selected in the twenty-fifth round of the 2002 amateur draft out of Hazelwood West High School in St. Louis County, and he turned down a scholarship offer from the University of Missouri to begin his pro career. Pitching for the Cardinals is an honor McClellan does not take lightly, and he knows how lucky he is to be playing major league baseball at all. He knows that if he acted conceited, or used his major league status to elevate himself above other people, he would be knocked down in a hurry.

"You don't go through this game for a very long period of time without getting a piece of the humble pie," McClellan said.

One such experience for McClellan came during the Cardinals' postseason run in 2011. He had been the pitcher who stepped into the starting rotation when Adam Wainwright went down with an elbow injury in spring training, and he stayed there until the end of July. He was 6–6 as a starter, with a respectable 4.21 ERA, but was moved to the bullpen for the rest of the season.

When the Cardinals reached the playoffs, McClellan found himself off the team's roster for the division series against the Phillies. He was added in time for the league championship series against the Brewers, but he pitched in only one game, lasting just one-third of an inning and giving up two hits and one run. When it came time for the team to set the roster for the World Series, McClellan was the odd man out again. It was a situation, he said, that would have been much tougher to deal with had he not become a better Christian over the preceding several years.

"It was not the most fun time for me personally," McClellan said. "Having a perspective on what's really important helps you get through that. Being able to keep the focus on the right things is something that always helps me get through some tough times."

And McClellan knew in his heart that even if he did not pitch in the World Series, he had played a role in getting there with his work both as a starter and reliever throughout the 2011 season. As he sat at his locker in July 2012 and knew he would not be able to pitch for the rest of the season, McClellan understood he was experiencing a different test of his faith, but one he trusted he could handle just as well.

"With where I am now in my faith and understanding and being able to see the big picture, I know that if my shoulder never heals or gets better it's not the end of the world," he said. "I don't wake up and determine whether I am going to have a good day or a bad day based on how I feel or the results of a game. That helps you stay even-keeled and gets you through life.

"You have success and failure lots of times in this game. You are not as good as you want to be, and I think if you measure yourself on a baseball standard I think you are doing yourself an injustice."

Not being able to pitch, and having to rehab his injury in hopes that he can pitch again in 2013, was not going to change McClellan's outlook on cheering on his teammates for the rest of the season and hoping they could earn a return trip to the postseason.

"I'm still a part of the team, and my job is to rehab and get better and be here for these guys and support them and be ready to go next year," he said. "I come in here and do my work and work harder than if I was playing. I let these guys know I am here to support them in any way I can."

That includes still putting on a uniform and sitting in the bullpen for several innings during every home game.

"I leave when it's time for them to go to work, and then I do what I need to do in treatment," he said.

One thing McClellan did not do following the July surgery was waste time worrying about his future. He knew he was eligible for arbitration before the 2013 season, and there was a possibility the Cardinals might not offer him a contract—exactly what did happen. He had heard similar talk last winter, and even the possibility that he might be traded, and decided not to become consumed by something that might never happen.

"The future is always one of those things which is out of your hands," McClellan said. "You know God has a place for you, and a plan for you, and you just have to trust in that whether it is here or wherever. It might not even be in baseball. Whatever it is, I'm at peace with that. I will be all right with it, and my family will be okay. We will be stronger by whatever happens.

"Obviously, this is the best situation for me and the best place to be, but that doesn't always mean that's where God wants you to be. It's comfortable for me, and sometimes that scares you, because a lot of times I don't think God wants you too comfortable. It's definitely been a growing experience and, luckily, where I am in my faith I have a good understanding that I can live with whatever happens and be okay with it."

Part of the reason that McClellan feels that way is now, at twenty-eight years old, he knows there will be a time in the not-too-distant future when playing baseball will be in his past, no matter what happens. He also believes he is a strong enough Christian that he realizes his family and God are far more important than baseball. He started realizing that a few years ago when someone once asked him if he prayed for a win before he went to the mound.

"I told him, 'I don't think God cares who wins or loses,'" McClellan said. "I say a prayer when I come in the game for strength and concentration and that's it. I don't pray for performance. The guy you are pitching against might be praying the same thing. I pray for those things He can give you, and ask that you play to the best of your ability."

Even though he was not pitching in the second half of the 2012 season, McClellan was still praying.

"I pray for health and direction and to get back healthy so I can play catch with my kids, even if I can't play baseball again," he said. "I want to be able to throw the football around. I feel like I will be in the right place and God's will will be guiding me through it."

As he has gotten older, McClellan has come to realize his relationship with God is far more important to him than whatever short-term success he has in baseball. That might be hard for some fans to understand, but it should be a reality for all players, McClellan said.

"The analogy I have used for years is that when I come home from a tough game, my dog is always excited to see me," he said. "She doesn't care if I blew the game or not. I like to use that same comparison to God. He doesn't care either way as long as you come home to Him; He's always excited to see you.

"It's a good vision to have, especially for late-inning relievers who are in a lot of close games. You give up a run and a lot of times it's the game. It's a comforting vision for me knowing, as I head home, that I can leave the game at the ballpark. I know there are about fifty thousand fans that are not too happy with me and more watching on television, but I am going home to the right people and the right mind-set."

McClellan does not want fans to misunderstand his statement and think that he doesn't care if he wins or loses a game.

"When we are out there, we are called to do the best we can," he said. "I want to compete as hard as I can and come out on the winning end. I just look at the fact there is a bigger picture. We are all called by God to do the best we can with the abilities that we have been given. It is our job to use those abilities in the right way."

Perhaps because of the injury, but also because of his increasing age, McClellan has started to think more about what his life will be like after his playing career is over.

"I think about it a lot," McClellan said. "Mike Matheny was one of the guys who challenged me a long time ago about focusing on something I want to do after baseball. In this game your career could be over at any point. It could be over today or ten years from now. My wife and I have talked about it, and we have some ideas, and one of those things will happen and we will put it into play and see where it takes us."

One thing McClellan will not worry about when his career is over is what kind of legacy he has left in the game.

"Will people twenty years from now know you and talk about you?" McClellan said. "My perspective is I really don't care. I'm not here to be a baseball player. I'm here to support my teammates, to open my eyes and be an example and to learn from people. If I do that, I don't care what my results are, and I don't care if I have a two-year career or a ten-year career.

"If I can go home at the end and say I had a meaningful career and spent my time wisely and did things I felt I needed to do from a Christian standpoint, I don't care what the baseball card says or what the wins and losses were. I think if you have that understanding, you don't really care how things turn out. I want to win, and we are called to do the best of our ability. But a lot of times the way we have it planned out is not the way it's supposed to be. That makes it easier to deal with."

One of the players who has helped McClellan come to grips with that reality is Adam Wainwright.

"Baseball is a unique environment," McClellan said. "It's a lot different than a nine-to-five job. We are a family, because we really do see each other more than our own families. Guys here lean on Adam a lot because he is a real mentor and a role model. I do, not only in baseball but in life.

"He is a guy who you can sit down and talk about issues with, and I'm not sure, but I don't think in a whole lot of other work environments you can do that. They don't have that close, family-type environment that we have. I definitely have grown spiritually because of the baseball environment."

More than one Cardinal shared McClellan's belief that part of the reason for the strong Christian bond on the team is all the activities that bring the players together to have those discussions, something he believes is missing on many other teams.

"When we have chapel, there will be twenty-plus guys in there," McClellan said. "When we had Bible study in spring training, we met at five thirty in the morning probably three times a week, and we usually had at least ten guys there—before a long day of spring training practice and a game. The guys on this team are committed to it, and it definitely is a growing process."

Part of the success, McClellan knows, is because it is the team leaders, such as Wainwright, Lance Berkman, and Matt Holliday, who are the most active leaders of the group. As young players come to the team and see those veterans participating, it is easy for them to jump on board without being ashamed or scared to express their religious beliefs.

"You have people here who are very accomplished," McClellan said. "Lance Berkman has done just about everything there is to do in this game. He can stand up and lead a chapel service or a Bible study. Here is a guy like that, who has had all the success he has had, and he doesn't forget what is the most important thing in his life and he isn't afraid to show it.

"It makes you try to measure up. This guy is reading his Bible every day and leading people, and he is about as successful as you can be. That makes you realize you still have a lot of work to do."

McClellan realized, as soon as he knew that his shoulder surgery was going to keep him off the field for the rest of the season, that he could still make a contribution to this team. On a team with many younger pitchers coming along, McClellan wanted to be there for them, and offer whatever suggestions and advice he could, and be there to answer questions as some older pitchers were there for him when he was first arriving in the major leagues.

Pitchers in the bullpen have a lot of time to talk before they have to go to work in the middle or late innings, and it is not unusual for religion to become one of the topics of the day.

"We've got something good going on here and it's something that doesn't just happen overnight," McClellan said. "It comes from a lot of quality people not afraid to stand up for what they believe in and talk about it."

One of the people who did that as a player was Matheny, McClellan said, and his leadership has continued since he became the team's manager.

"When he played here, he kind of changed the culture of the organization," McClellan said. "Wainwright followed, and the organization has gone out and got more good guys here. I wasn't here before [when Matheny played], but I have heard stories about how Mike was the one who saw to it that some changes were made in the way we do things.

"Mike to me is a big part of the way things are here. Tony [La Russa] was always great about it and never restricted us from doing anything. We could do whatever we needed to do. But having Mike sitting in that office, you know he is a guy you can go sit down with and talk to. I brought him down here a few times before he became our manager so he could participate in our studies just because I had that much respect for him. He's been a big mentor to me. Most of the times I sit down and talk with Mike, it has nothing to do with baseball."

That is one of the reasons, as he cheered on his teammates in the second half of the season, that McClellan was not worried about his future. He has left it in God's hands and knows He will take care of it.

"My favorite Bible verse is Romans 8:31, and when you think about it, you realize it is a verse that will allow you to understand how big of a thing it is that we are talking about. If you really believe, and know that God is on your side, there shouldn't be anything on the other side that can scare you.

"When you look back through the Scriptures and see all the challenges people had, when they fully believed and trusted in God, it always turned out to be okay. It didn't matter what they were doing or how big the battle was, they were able to survive it. That's something, which kind of lets you understand, and refreshes your memory, of how big and important this is.

"I don't know how long I am going to play baseball, or what God has in store for me. I know I am here for now and doing what He wants me to do, and I will do that until He changes it."

TEN

TREVOR ROSENTHAL

Do not be anxious about anything, but in every situation, by prayer and petition, with thanksgiving, present your requests to God. And the peace of God, which transcends all understanding, will guard your hearts and your minds in Christ Jesus.

—Philippians 4:6–7 NIV

Trevor Rosenthal was trying to catch his breath. As he stood on the mound at Milwaukee's Miller Park on July 18, there was a reason the twenty-two-year-old right-handed pitcher was nervous.

Making his major league debut in the eighth inning, with the Cardinals trailing 4–2, Rosenthal had walked the first batter he faced, Nyjer Morgan, then allowed a single. After throwing a called third strike past Corey Hart, and then getting the second out of the inning on a lineout, Rosenthal issued another walk to load the bases.

Another pitcher was warming up in the bullpen. Rosenthal saw manager Mike Matheny climb the steps and head out of the St. Louis dugout, walking toward the mound.

"Anytime you see the manager coming to the mound, you don't expect that when he leaves the mound you are still going to be in the game," said Rosenthal.

As Matheny reached the mound, Rosenthal held out the baseball. Instead of taking it from the young pitcher, however, Matheny stopped him as Rosenthal started to walk off the mound.

"You've worked all your life to get to this moment, haven't you?" Matheny asked Rosenthal. "I just wanted to come out here and enjoy the moment with you. Now go get this guy."

The reassuring message helped calm Rosenthal's nerves. He struck out Chris Gomez to get out of the inning and was congratulated by Matheny as he reached the dugout.

"That was a special experience, a really cool moment," Rosenthal said. "I felt he trusted me that I could get out of the jam I had put myself into, and luckily I was able to do that."

Rosenthal knew he probably would have more time to reflect on his major league debut, which turned out to be the start of a magical rookie season with the Cardinals. The year was, in a word, a whirlwind.

The year began with a nonroster invitation to spring training. Matheny had the idea that he wanted some of the promising young pitchers in the farm system to be exposed to the major leaguers. He put those pitchers in groups, where they basically shadowed pitchers such as Chris Carpenter, Adam Wainwright, and Kyle Lohse through the early camp drills.

Whatever Carpenter or Wainwright was doing, Rosenthal was expected to do the same thing. He took a small notebook onto the field with him and jotted down notes that he wanted to remember. He asked questions not just about on-field matters but about how the veterans handled off-field issues as well.

"The experience is second to none," Rosenthal said at the time. "I've been able to learn so much in such a short period of time. I'm just trying to soak it all in and remember it. We've talked about a lot of little things, pointers that could eventually change how your season goes. They offer a lot of insight, and it's not always with words, watching how they go about their job. When you are not doing what they think you should be doing, they definitely tell us about it. You can tell there is a certain expectation that they want us to meet."

After spring training came a jump from low Class A Quad Cities, where Rosenthal had pitched in 2011, to Springfield, skipping the high Class A level—a major promotion for a player who was not a top draft pick. In seventeen starts at Springfield, Rosenthal was 8–6 with an impressive 2.78 ERA, less than two years removed from pitching for Cowley County Community College in Arkansas City, Kansas. It was there the Cardinals discovered Rosenthal and made him their twenty-first-round selection in the 2009 draft, the 639th player picked that year.

The story of how Rosenthal ended up falling to the Cardinals in that draft, and beginning his rapid ascension to the major leagues, is another example of how all it takes is an opportunity, and then it's what an individual does with it that counts. Aaron Looper, a former major league pitcher and the cousin of Cardinals' former number-one draft pick Braden Looper, was the area scout responsible for finding and recommending Rosenthal. The grand total of times he saw Rosenthal pitch that spring? One time, for a total of one inning.

"I heard through the grapevine that he had been up to 95 [mph] and was definitely a guy who had a little bit of buzz at the end of the year," Looper said. "I went to the Kansas Juco regional tournament because I thought it would be my last chance to see him. I sat on him for three games before he finally got in to pitch one inning and that was it.

"I know it sounds crazy, but I put a gut feel on him after one inning. I think he topped off at 94 when I was there. He had a good arm and was a projectable kid. The main thing that stuck out for me was his limited experience and how he went after hitters. He wasn't intimidated, and he threw strikes. That's not easy to do when you are just beginning to pitch."

Each of the Cardinals' area scouts is allowed three "gut-feel" stickers, which they can place on the players they recommend for the draft. Those are usually reserved for players who can be selected in the fifth round or much later, prospects who usually have not been exposed to multiple scouts from the organization.

"He was one of my three that year," Looper said. "I still thought somebody probably had seen him more and [had] more history with him and would probably take him before we had that opportunity," Looper said. "I thought he would go right about the tenth round. He just kept sliding in the draft and, fortunately for us, we got him when we did.

"There are just a handful of guys you feel good about as far as prospects. The gut-feel stickers are something to help their magnets (on the draft board) stand out a little bit and maybe you will have a better chance of drafting them. Trevor was a tricky situation because I had no history with him. He deserves all of the credit, obviously. I wish I was a good enough scout to tell you that I thought he would be doing what he did in St. Louis, but I can't tell you that."

Rosenthal had played shortstop before starting to pitch in the middle of his freshman year. He had not been drafted out of high school, and really emerged for the Cowley County Tigers as the spring of 2009 went along. Twelve players from that team were named to the conference's first team, second team, or honorable mention, and Rosenthal was not one of them.

He pitched a total of twenty-nine innings that season, going 1–0 with eight saves. He had a 2.40 ERA, striking out 41 and walking 14.

As the second day of the draft got underway that June day

in 2009, Looper had the list of players he had recommended to the Cardinals in front of him. It was his second draft as a scout, getting back into the game after his playing career had ended. As the rounds started to drop, and Rosenthal's name was still on the board, he got more excited.

"I called him and told him I thought it looked like we were going to have a chance to get him," Looper said. "I think he was mowing the yard at the time. After the draft I drove up to Lee's Summit and talked with him and his parents and a couple or three weeks later we got him signed."

Rosenthal was the first player Looper signed as a scout, so Looper naturally followed Rosenthal's progress in the minor leagues. Looper did not see him again in person until watching him pitch an inning in the Texas League All-Star game, shortly before he was promoted to the Cardinals.

"He's been so much fun to watch," Looper said. "Some of those guys, the pressure just seems to make them better, and it seems like that's what it's done for him.

"I don't believe he knew how good an arm he had. He knew he threw hard, but I don't think it was until he got into pro baseball that he thought he had a chance to do it for a long time and be pretty good at it. The coaches deserve credit for making him realize his potential, but the rest of it is on Trevor. It's amazing how quickly he did it.

"It's a great story to tell guys. If you work hard and trust your gut, you might fall into some decent players."

Rosenthal's selection and signing with the Cardinals did not create headlines. He began his professional career in virtual anonymity. Coming into the 2011 season, he was not ranked as one of the top thirty prospects in the organization by *Baseball America*. By June 2012, just a year and a couple of months later, however, the magazine said he deserved to be included with Shelby

Miller and Carlos Martinez as the best pitching prospects in the Cardinals' farm system.

Rosenthal had always believed in himself and his talent, but the promotion to St. Louis still happened so quickly that he was not prepared for it. A few months earlier he had been in a low Class A league. For a player without faith, it would have been easy to get a big head and act conceited at the promotion, but Rosenthal would not let that happen. His quick success, if anything, has only increased his belief of the importance of faith.

"I've found out how much more important faith is," he said. "When you have situations change, and have to make a lot of adjustments, a strong faith helps. It keeps me in check and keeps me humble and on track. You don't get diverted by outside distractions."

One of the other reasons Rosenthal is more grounded than most twenty-two-year-olds who suddenly find themselves in the major leagues is the fact that he is married. He and his wife, Lindsey, were married in December 2011. The couple met in Johnson City, Tennessee, in 2010 when Rosenthal was pitching in rookie ball and she was in nursing school.

"I grew up in a Christian home, but when I was young I was not completely into it," Rosenthal said. "But as I got older, and met Lindsey, I was able to make it my own and knew I was going to make it a big part of my life."

While Rosenthal did not have doubts about his faith or his marriage, he did have some concerns about his baseball future, specifically if he might be better off pursuing a different career.

"The odds of making it in this game are so slim, that I knew they were pretty much against me," Rosenthal said. "Realizing I wanted to eventually have kids and a family, I just wanted to make sure I would be in a position to provide for them and do that."

The day never came, however, when Rosenthal decided to

abandon his dreams of becoming a major leaguer, and he is glad now that he stuck with it.

"Anything I do I am going to give it my all," he said. "There really wasn't ever a decision. I just never did anything else. I never felt strongly enough that this was something I shouldn't be doing."

The challenges have changed over the years for Rosenthal. One of his concerns now is the schedule of a major leaguer, which requires him to spend so much time away from his new wife. That has only increased his desire to succeed, and to become a better Christian at the same time.

"I'm lucky to be blessed with talent, and I want to make the most of it," Rosenthal said. "I've worked hard to get here. Everybody that gets drafted has the talent to get here, but it's just about putting in the work necessary to make it happen."

When the Cardinals drafted him, Rosenthal had to decide if he wanted to sign then or return to school for another year and try to improve his draft position. He decided to sign, and he has had no regrets.

"Every game is exciting and memorable," he said. "It started in spring training, when I was facing guys and I was like, 'Oh, man.'"

Then Rosenthal realized he had a job to do and tried to block out the fact that he was pitching against some of the players he had watched in the major leagues for years. Two of his favorite players growing up in Kansas City were Albert Pujols, who went to high school not far from Rosenthal's home, and Zack Greinke, a star with the hometown Royals. The fact that Rosenthal was now at the same level with them, in the majors, really was hard for him to believe.

Others, however, quickly grasped the fact that he had the talent and deserved to be there when they saw him perform on the mound. Because of a numbers situation, Rosenthal ended up going back and forth from St. Louis to Memphis a couple of times during the season. He came back up to the Cardinals to stay at the end of August, and his regular-season totals showed the potential to become a star—in 19 games, covering a total of 22²/₃ innings, Rosenthal allowed just 14 hits and 7 walks while striking out 25, many on fastballs clocked at close to 100 miles per hour.

During September, as the Cardinals' bullpen settled into an orderly progression, manager Mike Matheny increasingly relied on him to come into a jam in the middle innings, and Rosenthal was usually able to get out of it. He did not allow any of six inherited runners to score, and he finished the season with seven consecutive scoreless outings.

"He's made the most of his opportunities," Matheny said. "We've needed him to step in and pitch some big innings."

Rosenthal planned to continue his education over the winter, moving to St. Louis so he could work out with some of the team's veteran pitchers, especially Carpenter. In addition to putting in a lot of effort on the baseball side, Rosenthal has tried to improve himself through educating his mind and reading a lot of books, especially self-improvement books and books about learning how to be mentally tough, which is especially important in the game of baseball.

"I also was reading some doctors' books, since that is my wife's field, and I want to be able to understand the lingo and what she is talking about," Rosenthal said. "I was interested in the medical field coming out of high school, but then my passion for baseball took over and that kind of went aside. I love talking to my wife about what she does."

Another book he has spent a lot of time reading and talking about with Lindsey is the Bible.

"I try to [read the Bible] multiple times a day on my own and then with my wife at night," he said. "I skip around and find something interesting, and that helps us grow and build our faith together."

As a baseball player, Rosenthal settled on his favorite Bible verse—Philippians 4:13—a long time ago. It is one he thinks about every time he steps on the mound, knowing Christ is the source of his strength.

"It's my go-to verse," Rosenthal said, "especially during the season. I go back to that, and realize that everything is going to be all right."

ELEVEN

SKIP SCHUMAKER

A man's heart deviseth his way: but the LORD directeth his steps.

—Proverbs 16:9 KJV

The schedule called for the Cardinals to have a night off on July 19, a welcome break after a tough six-game trip to Cincinnati and Milwaukee to open the second half of the season. They might not have been at Busch Stadium playing a game that evening, but this was far from a night off for Skip Schumaker and more than half of his teammates.

Instead, they were on hand at a fund-raising event at the SunRise United Methodist Church in suburban O'Fallon, Missouri, all there because of a one-year-old girl named Reesa who lived in Arizona. Four months earlier, Reesa had been diagnosed with a rare disease, Krabbe leukodystrophy, which has no cure and is generally fatal within two years. Schumaker had begun planning and organizing the event from the moment he received the phone call about Reesa's condition from her father, Sean Stutzman—Schumaker's best friend.

"That was a tough phone call, one I wish I could forget about but I won't forget," Schumaker said. "It's going to be the most difficult two years of their lives, and not a fun time for their friends either."

Stutzman and Schumaker grew up down the street from one another in Orange County, California, and were baseball teammates at Aliso Niguel High School. Schumaker moved to the area when he was in eighth grade, and the two were together through high school before they went their separate ways in college, Schumaker to Cal State–Santa Barbara and Stutzman to Arizona State. They still remained close. Each was the best man in the other's wedding, one of the reasons Schumaker was happy and excited when he found out the previous fall the Stutzmans were expecting their first child. As the married father of two healthy children, Schumaker knew how much having a baby would change Stutzman's life.

That feeling changed with the telephone call informing Schumaker about Reesa's disease, and unfortunately for Schumaker, it was the second difficult phone call he had received that spring. About two weeks earlier he had received the devastating news that another friend, the wife of another high school teammate, Jody Weisberg, had died during childbirth at a hospital in Mission Viejo, California. Megan Weisberg was only thirty-one years old when she died on March 15. Jody Weisberg suddenly became a single parent to two little boys. "Megan had a blood clot while she was giving birth," Schumaker said. "Jody was in the room, and one minute they went from having the best minute of their life giving birth to her being dead. It was tough on everybody. I had known her forever. Those couple of experiences back-to-back really changed me forever."

The baby boy, Tosh, was born during an emergency C-section and was without oxygen for more than a minute. Doctors initially did not know if he would survive, and he ended up spending three months in intensive care. There is still a chance, Schumaker said, that he could suffer from cerebral palsy.

So that spring Schumaker was thinking far more about his friends than about the game of baseball, organizing fund-raisers not only for Reesa but also for Weisberg to help with his high medical bills.

"What has happened in my life this year has been a life-changing experience for me in terms of what's really important," Schumaker said. "I feel baseball has given me a platform to help out other people more than ever.

"Those two experiences back-to-back really tested my faith. You wonder why bad things happen to good people, and you realize you have to have faith in God's timing. I know, in Reesa's short time, she has affected more people than I have in thirty-two years of living. There's a reason for everything."

After learning of Reesa's illness, Schumaker set out not only to organize the July event to help raise money for her care but also to raise awareness of the disease and to encourage states to have newborn babies tested for it, when they can still be treated.

"I feel like this is my responsibility," Schumaker said. "Not too many people can go out in the community and be in this position. I couldn't have gotten this whole thing together without playing for the Cardinals and the support this community has toward its players. I felt like maybe I could do something to help, but the response has been above and beyond what I could have imagined."

Many of Schumaker's teammates agreed to come to the church and sign autographs, with all of the money going to Baby Reesa's foundation. Many former Cardinals came too, as did members of the St. Louis Rams and St. Louis Blues. Auction items arrived from country music stars Garth Brooks, Taylor Swift, and others. Fifteen Cardinals showed up that night, including manager Mike Matheny, many staying well past the one hour they had agreed to be there because the lines of fans seeking autographs were so long. When the event was over, Schumaker found out they had raised more than $100,000. Earlier, Matheny had told Schumaker he also was donating half of the proceeds of his annual golf tournament to the cause.

"Living in California, I wouldn't be able to do this," Schumaker said. "This is strictly because I play here that I am able to do it."

Schumaker has realized over the years how lucky he is to play in St. Louis for other reasons, including the fact that it helped him become a Christian. Growing up in Southern California, Schumaker had very supporting and loving parents, but religion was not a central focus in their home.

"Knowing what I do now, I wish I had it as part of my life growing up," Schumaker said. "Still, I had a great childhood with wonderful parents."

It wasn't until 2005, when he reached Triple-A Memphis, that Schumaker was first introduced to what being a Christian could offer to him. His introduction came from teammate Adam Wainwright.

"We became best friends in Triple-A and our wives became really good friends," Schumaker said. "He introduced [Christianity] to me, but he didn't force it on me. He never pressured me. He asked me to go certain places with him, and to do certain things with him, but he let me learn on my own. If I had questions, he was always there to answer them."

Wainwright said the conversations between him and Schumaker covered myriad subjects, and hundreds of hours, mostly while at the same time playing Xbox or cards in a hotel room.

"One thing you have to know about the minor leagues is there are long bus trips, hotels that do not have huge bars, and are in towns that, for the most part, do not have happening areas to go to after games," Wainwright said. "So what happens a lot of times is that you get together in rooms. You play video games or play cards. We played a lot of poker. Skip would come over to my room and we played Xbox."

Somewhere before, during, or after their Mario Kart or RBI Baseball contests, the two would get into lengthy and involved conversations. They were building friendship and trust.

"He and I talked about everything except religion," Wainwright said. "We were constantly hanging out after every game, before games, during games. That year we really gained ground as friends and got really close. We built a relationship as friends first, and I think that's the best way to do it when introducing something as big as God. You need to have some even terms there, and respect. That's what it really takes to spread the Word."

As their conversations gradually turned toward God, Wainwright began to quiz Schumaker about what he thought the Bible said about a situation, or who he thought Jesus was—real, fundamental Christian questions. Wainwright was a believer, but a relatively new one, and someone with admittedly more questions than answers himself. He had the foundation of having been brought up in a church environment, which gave him the edge in knowledge about God.

"Skip was a big-time skeptic," Wainwright said. "He had an open mind, and he was not an atheist or a nonbeliever. He was just somebody who didn't know about it.

"There were times when Skip and I would end a talk and he would say, 'I just don't know if this is for me. I don't know if I can do this.' I just kept praying that if God was meant to be in his life, He would reveal himself to him through one of our conversations or somewhere else."

Schumaker admits he was skeptical at first, and he did ask a lot of questions. One of the facts about having faith, Wainwright assured him, was that it was okay to question God and to not understand everything.

"I still have questions today," Schumaker said. "I don't think that ever leaves. You can look at all of the great things God has given you, but when a couple of bad things happen all of a sudden, it's easy to think, *There is no such thing as God.* The only time I question God is when really bad things happen. That's what is tough sometimes, and nobody can really explain it except for the big guy upstairs."

When he was a new Christian, Schumaker said he often used his faith as a way to bargain with God.

"If I went to a charity event, then I thought I should get four hits the next day," Schumaker said. "That's how I thought it should work. I've learned that's not how it works. I have to give thanks, no matter what, for this opportunity."

When he was a student with Stutzman and Weisberg at Aliso Niguel High School, baseball was the most important activity in Schumaker's world. He wanted to play major league baseball from the time he was a youngster, but not blessed with great physical size, he knew the only way he was going to succeed was if he outworked everybody else. So that was what he did. He became a good enough player in high school to earn All-State honors and receive a college scholarship. He became good enough in college to be selected by the Cardinals in the fifth round of the 2001 amateur draft.

Schumaker was an outfielder then, and he began his climb through the minor leagues, reaching the Double-A level in only two years. Two years later he found himself making his major league debut, and after shuttling back and forth between Triple-A and the major leagues, he was in the majors to stay in 2008.

It's probably not a coincidence that his ascent to the major leagues coincided with the birth of his son, Brody, in November 2007. That was the moment, he says, when God, faith, and his life all were magically linked together. Schumaker and his wife,

Lindsey, had been trying to have a baby for a few years, but she had suffered multiple miscarriages, and the couple had doubts whether she would ever be able to have a child.

"That's when it all clicked," he said. "I saw him pop out and I know that doesn't just happen. That miracle can only happen from one person. It didn't make any sense. I already was a believer at the time, but that was when I knew."

After playing regularly in the outfield for the Cardinals in 2008, Schumaker had another challenge placed on his plate by manager Tony La Russa, who asked the career outfielder to learn to play second base, a transition that does not occur very often. It is much more common for an infielder to become an outfielder rather than the other way around. Schumaker was determined to prove he could do it, however, and as soon as he learned about La Russa's plan, he picked up his glove, went over to his high school field, and had his dad hit him grounder after grounder to begin getting ready for his new assignment. For the next two years, Schumaker became the Cardinals' primary second baseman and did a solid job.

In November 2009, the Schumakers had another baby, this time a girl, Presley. Schumaker was more committed than ever to make certain both children were raised in a Christian home.

"They are going to learn early about Jesus and what He can do," Schumaker said. "That's one of my main goals, having Him as part of our house early in their lives."

Every time he looks at his wife and two healthy kids, Schumaker knows God has blessed him. And that makes him think again about Reesa, and about his friend Jody and their struggles.

"You almost feel bad that you have a beautiful wife and two healthy kids," Schumaker said. "You wonder 'why me?' sometimes. That's why I know I have to get more involved.

"To have something like this happen to a kid is rough for me to figure out. I can deal with people dying when they are in their seventies and eighties. But for a horrible illness to happen to a kid is tough. I think there are roughly twenty kids a year diagnosed with [Reesa's disease]. It's like a one in two hundred million chance. You have a better chance of winning the lottery."

Schumaker can see the "why me?" parallels between having healthy or sick children and having the ability and opportunity to play major league baseball or not. He believes he was handpicked by God because of the opportunity he has to help others and to try to make a difference. And as much as he wanted to succeed on the baseball field for the Cardinals in 2012, he admits what happened to him off the field was far more significant.

The 2012 season already promised to be a transition year for Schumaker anyway, well before baby Reesa's disease was diagnosed or Megan Weisberg died. He had signed a contract to return to the Cardinals, knowing he probably would play less than he did in 2011, when he started eighty-nine games at second base and another five games in the outfield.

"I understood through negotiations that I was going to be the utility guy, that I was going to play when somebody else needed a day off," Schumaker said. "They wanted to give Tyler Greene a chance to play. I was okay with it. I told my agent I wanted to be here, and I was not going to listen to anybody else. I wanted to be here.

"I have a tightness with this community and I knew that my faith wouldn't wander if I was with this central corps of guys here, and that was important to me. Money isn't everything. My family is happy and I'm happy. That has not changed.

"The group of guys we have here, with Adam, Lance Berkman, Matt Holliday, those guys are as good as it gets."

Schumaker has played with dozens of players, Christians and

non-Christians, throughout his career. For him, the biggest difference between the two does not happen on the field but occurs off the field.

"For me, more than anything else, [it's] about being known for the type of person you are, not what you do for work," he said. "I hate being defined as a baseball player. I want to be defined for what you do for the community, for Jesus, and for everything else. The main thing for me this year is trying to be defined as the person instead of coming off a World Series title as a baseball player."

In 2012, Schumaker started sixty-eight games, either at second base or in the outfield, and hit .290 in those games. He was a valuable member of the bench when he was not starting. Schumaker admits he has learned a lot from all of his teammates, both about baseball and about life. He is becoming more comfortable talking about his faith, but he admits there is still a lot he doesn't know.

"If people ask, I will let them know," he said. "I'm not as much a student as Lance is, and I am not as comfortable answering certain questions because I may not know all of the answers. I'm studying to get that way, but will I ever get to where Lance is? I'm not sure."

Where Schumaker is, however, is at a realization that God put him on the Cardinals for the 2012 season to be able to use that platform as a way to help others, specifically baby Reesa and other children afflicted with Krabbe disease, which affects the central nervous system. Before Schumaker got involved with raising funds for Baby Reesa and increasing awareness of the disease, he had never heard of the condition, like most of the general public except for those whose lives had been affected by it.

The Missouri legislature had passed a bill in 2009 requiring the testing of all newborn babies for Krabbe disease and other childhood diseases. A three-year period was established to allow for the law to be implemented, primarily to give time for the testing equipment, training, and finances to be put in place. The law was named "Brady's law" after a baby named Brady Cunningham who died from the disease in 2009.

Schumaker met Brady's relatives at the Baby Reesa fundraiser in July, and he also found out that even though the three-year wait was over, the law had not gone into effect as scheduled on July 1, 2012. Even worse, two of the diseases in the leukodystrophy family, which were supposed to have been included in the new testing procedures—Krabbe disease and Niemann Pick disease—had been taken off the list. That decision apparently was made because the company the state was using had not developed a test for those two diseases. When Schumaker heard what had happened, he wanted to know what he could do to help.

"I was going to get involved and call the governor if I needed to, but it kind of grew legs on its own because of the awareness created by the Cardinals community," Schumaker said. "They had brushed it aside. The governor didn't think it was necessary. Enough people were moved by Reesa's story, and more and more people started talking about it."

One of the people who heard the story was the director of the health department in the city of St. Louis. When the medical personnel got involved, a new company was found that did have the proper equipment to administer the necessary tests. Schumaker soon got the news from Stutzman that the testing was now being conducted. Every baby born in the state gets a "blood spot" from their heel sent to the health lab in Jefferson City. Tests can reveal if a baby is afflicted with any of those five diseases.

"Newborn screening is huge," Schumaker said. "It can prevent people from going through some horrible, horrible things in life that they shouldn't have to go through. It's something that can be prevented, and the fact this law was passed says a lot for what Reesa has done in her short time here."

If a baby tests positive for Krabbe disease as a newborn, there is a cure. The child can undergo either a cord blood or bone marrow transplant if the condition is detected within the first two weeks of life. After that, it generally is too late. The relatives of Brady Cunningham are convinced that Schumaker's involvement helped finally make the tests a reality.

"Skip played a major role in it," said Jessy Cunningham. "When someone from the Cardinals says something, people will listen. This just shows who Skip is and what he's all about. God puts people in your path for certain things. It was God's plan. I think God used Skip to help accomplish it."

Through all of his trying experiences during the year—concluding with his trade to the Dodgers in December—Schumaker knows one fact is indisputable: how much his faith has grown.

"My faith is 100 percent stronger," Schumaker said. "This is how faith works. It finally is hitting home for me."

It hits home for Wainwright, too, when he sees Schumaker now and remembers the young, uncertain man he became friends with seven years ago in the minor leagues.

"You're talking about a guy who has one of the biggest hearts I have ever encountered from anyone," Wainwright said. "He's a guy you could trust with your life, a guy you could leave your kids with and go out of town and know they are being taken care of, watched after, and brought up the way you want them brought up.

"It just shows you how great God is. No one is untouchable. You see the way Skip lives, and you are seeing the fruits of the Spirit. This off-season he called me several times, super excited about some awesome things he was doing for children and for

Jesus. We're talking about a guy who three or four years ago maybe wouldn't go into chapel.

"Skip and I are as close as two guys can possibly be in faith, and in growing in our faith. And we are seeing some great things happening."

One of those things was Schumaker being nominated as the National League Central's candidate for the Marvin Miller Man of the Year Award, which is presented by the major league Players Association to honor a player who "inspires others to higher levels of achievement by their on-field performances and contributions to their communities." A vote of MLB players determines the winner.

But Schumaker did not get involved in all of his charity efforts in 2012 to win an award. He just thought it was the right thing to do.

"My favorite Bible verse is Proverbs 16:9: 'A man's heart plans his way, but the Lord directs his steps,'" Schumaker said. "You can plan on having a 3-for-4 game, or hit two home runs, every day, and you can plan on having a healthy family. All those are great things but ultimately it's not up to you 100 percent. That's why you have to have faith in Him for your career, your family, and everything else."

TWELVE

MITCHELL BOGGS

Therefore, since we have been justified through faith, we have peace
with God through our Lord Jesus Christ, through whom we have gained
access by faith into this grace in which we now stand. And we boast
in the hope of the glory of God. Not only so, but we also glory in our
sufferings, because we know that suffering produces perseverance;
perseverance, character; and character, hope. And hope does not put
us to shame, because God's love has been poured out into our hearts
through the Holy Spirit, who has been given to us.

—Romans 5:1–5 NIV

The streak began innocently enough. On June 14, Mitchell Boggs
trotted in from the Cardinals' bullpen to face Paul Konerko of the
Chicago White Sox with two outs in the top of the eighth inning.
Four pitches later, Boggs got Konerko to pop out to shortstop
Rafael Furcal, and his night was finished. One inning later, the
Cardinals had a 5–3 victory.

That short outing turned out to be the first of twenty-three
consecutive appearances in which Boggs did not give up a run—a
stretch that lasted almost two months, through August 5. He

appeared in all of those games between the seventh and ninth innings, becoming an important part of the team's bullpen.

It was a huge difference from the 2011 season, a year in which Boggs filled a number of different roles, including a short stint as the team's closer. It was a year that even featured a short demotion to the minor leagues. It was a year, Boggs said, that provided the biggest test to his faith since he started playing baseball.

"It was one of the worst experiences of my life playing baseball," Boggs said. "Still, I knew everything was going to be okay—even when I was in Triple-A and was not where I wanted to be. I had a lot of questions about my career and my standing in this organization, but I was at total peace with it. It was eye-opening to me. A lot of it had to do with my wife and parents supporting me. The most important thing was my faith—you know that if things don't go the way you want them to, there is a reason why it is happening. I hit rock bottom as far as my baseball career was concerned.

"It was one of the worst seasons of my life but also was one of the greatest growing experiences I've ever had. I had a lot of peace in the off-season and knew I was preparing myself and working as hard as I could to do the best that I could. I had a lot of questions heading into spring training. But I was at total peace. I know God has blessed me with incredible ability that I can go out and be great, if I put my faith and trust in Him. This game can really beat you down. Having that faith has really been a strength for me."

Boggs arrived in Florida in February 2012 not knowing what new manager Mike Matheny was expecting from him. He quickly found out.

One of Matheny's first acts after the pitchers and catchers reported was to calls Boggs into his office for a private talk, letting him know that everything that had happened in 2011 was history. The manager said he believed in Boggs's ability and planned to use him in late-inning, high-leverage situations in front of closer Jason Motte.

"It certainly gave me a reason to believe in myself a little bit more," Boggs said. "It's fun to go out and help us win, to be a guy who is counted on."

Boggs knows there were times earlier in his career when he would have reacted much differently to his struggles in 2011, which could have kept him from celebrating the World Series triumph with his teammates and might have changed his 2012 outlook as well.

"My wife can attest to the fact that I used to be very indulged in my performance," Boggs said. "If I was pitching well, I was a lot of fun to be around. I was always talking to everyone, calling home, everything was great. At other times, when things got tough for me and if I wasn't throwing the way I wanted to, I would kind of go into a little shelter—'Why is this happening?'—and start to get bitter. That's where my faith became really important to me and made me realize this is a game.

"There's a sense of peace that no matter what happens, if you go out there and perform the way you want or you don't, I know there is a greater importance to my life than throwing a baseball. That is something that is big to me. You deal with failure so much in this game that you can let it define you, and that's where a lot of guys get in trouble. For me, my faith has always let me know that there are bigger and more important things out there."

Boggs's faith formed as a young boy growing up in a Christian home in Dalton, Georgia. A talented high school quarterback as well as a pitcher, Boggs was one of those gifted prep athletes who had a choice to make of which sport he wanted to pursue. Boggs's ability as a topflight prep quarterback is an occasional point of discussion within the Cardinals' clubhouse, with other players wanting to know who was better, him or Matt Holliday.

As a senior at Dalton High School in 2001, Boggs led the Catamounts to the Class 4A state championship game, but their bid to win the school's first title since 1967 ended with a loss to Statesboro.

"Matt got all the accolades, but anybody who knows me knows I am pretty prideful of my high school football exploits," Boggs said. "I will never back down from that."

Boggs's love of football was what made it such a dilemma as to which sport to play in college, a decision he juggled for years. First he went to the University of Georgia to play baseball, playing in ten games as a freshman. He then transferred to the University of Tennessee at Chattanooga to play quarterback, but appeared in only three games, and halfway through the season realized he wanted to go back to Georgia and play baseball. The coach put him back on the team, and he was there in time for the preseason workouts.

"Football was a great experience for me when I was in high school," Boggs said at the time. "Me leaving Georgia in the beginning didn't have anything to do with baseball. I just wanted to find out if football was right for me."

Boggs said that he knew then if he continued playing football in college he would probably be coaching a high school team now instead of playing for the Cardinals.

"That would have been fine with me," Boggs said. "But [playing baseball] was something I really wanted to try because I knew if I didn't I probably would have regretted it for a long time.

"After I transferred, a lot of people wondered what I was doing, and then when I transferred back to Georgia to play baseball people wondered what I was doing. I have no regrets. I have peace with the decisions I made."

Two people who didn't wonder about his decisions, because they had been with him every step of his life, were Boggs's parents.

"I was fortunate to have parents who made my faith a priority," Boggs said. "Their faith set a pretty strong example for me to follow. To this day, they are the two people in this world that I have the most respect for because of their beliefs and character, the way they raised me and my brother."

It was that upbringing that prepared Boggs for the first challenges to his faith, which came, as it does for most young adults, when he went off to college.

"When you go to college, it's the first time you are off by yourself and that's when you find out who you are," Boggs said. "My faith had always been important to me growing up, but I didn't realize how important until I got out on my own. There were times when I absolutely leaned on my faith.

"It was very easy for me to have a strong faith growing up because of the leadership of my parents and my older brother. They set an incredible example. When you get out on your own, you realize things in life are not always going to go your way, and there is not always going to be somebody there looking out for you. Those are the times you realize how truly important your faith is."

Boggs got his chance to play baseball professionally when he was selected by the Cardinals in the fifth round of the 2005 draft. He was assigned to their short-season team in New Jersey in the New York–Penn League, where he went 4–4 in fifteen games. That season was followed by a year in Palm Beach; then he spent time in Springfield, Missouri, in Double-A before he reached Triple-A Memphis. There were numerous tests to Boggs's faith over those years.

"When you are playing the game off by yourself in the minor leagues, riding buses, living in obscure towns, you wonder a lot why you are doing this and if it's going to all work out," Boggs said. "You have a lot of questions and doubts, and those were times for me when my faith had its greatest importance."

Boggs realized early in his life and career that his faith was not going to be a major factor in whether he succeeded or failed on the baseball field. God had given him the ability to play the game, but he knew the results were dictated by other factors.

"I'm not one of those guys who believes that their faith dictates whether I am going to be successful or not," he said. "God has given me the ability to play this game, and it's my job to go out there and do the best I can. I do know that, because of my faith, I have peace with whatever happens. That's something I didn't have in the past.

"When you are only worried about success or failure, that makes it hard. This year, when I hit some rough spots, it was easier to bounce back."

Boggs did not believe the 2012 season could possibly be worse for him than 2011. The endorsement from the manager in spring training helped reassure him, even though he knew there were a lot of questions surrounding what he would do, and what his role would be, on the team.

"I knew I was not really on the radar as far as somebody the fan base believed in as a guy who could come in and do a huge part for the team," Boggs said. "But I just knew that even if it didn't work out the way I wanted it to, it was going to work out the way it was supposed to."

Luckily for Boggs and the Cardinals, the way he wanted the season to go, and the way it was supposed to go, turned out to be pretty much one and the same. He knew one of the biggest reasons was the confidence Matheny had placed in him during the spring, before he had even thrown one pitch in the bullpen.

"There was no excuse for Mitchell Boggs not to be more effective," Matheny told the *St. Louis Post-Dispatch* during the season. "We were intentional in telling him that we believe in him. The stuff, the makeup, the toughness, everything was there."

Boggs pitched in seventy-eight games during the season, and only three pitchers in the National League appeared more often, all pitching in eighty games. He earned a "hold" (where he protected a St. Louis lead) in thirty-four games, the most in the league and also a franchise record. He allowed only 6 of 35 inherited runners to score, and he retired the first batter he faced 62 times in his 78 appearances, an important statistic for a relief pitcher. He held opponents to a .211 batting average and allowed only 12 earned runs.

"This was a fun year," Boggs said. "I just tried to show up every day and be ready to pitch."

At no point in the season was that more evident than during his scoreless streak between June 14 and August 5. After giving up a two-run homer to the Chicago White Sox's A.J. Pierzynski on June 12, one of only five home runs Boggs allowed during the season, Boggs was not thinking about anything except getting the next hitter out when he came in to pitch to Konerko two days later.

It was, in fact, well into the streak before Boggs even realized he had not allowed a run for a while—including the entire month of July, when he pitched in thirteen of the Cardinals' twenty-five games during the month. In the combined months of June and July, Boggs walked only 3 batters in 22 innings and had an ERA of 1.23. Two of the three runs he allowed over those twenty-five games came on the Pierzynski home run.

"I'm not going to dwell on the things I do the day before or the week before, good or bad," Boggs said during the streak. "It doesn't help me. I've been there before."

Boggs knew the streak would eventually come to an end, and it did, on August 8 against the San Francisco Giants. The Cardinals were already losing 11–0 when Boggs was called on to pitch the ninth inning because some of the relievers who normally might have been used in such a position were unavailable. Boggs came into the game and gave up a grand slam to Marco Scutaro. The Giants' 15–0 win was the most lopsided shutout loss the Cardinals had suffered at home since 1961.

Boggs was just glad the runs he allowed were not the difference between a victory and a defeat for the Cardinals.

The next day he was back on the mound again, called upon to protect a 3–1 St. Louis lead against the Giants. He did so, retiring Melky Cabrera, Buster Posey, and Hunter Pence on eleven pitches.

"I know that [Matheny] believes in me," Boggs said earlier in the year. "I know that he supports me. That means a lot to me. It's good to know every day that the guy you're showing up to battle for believes in you."

Those games came at the point during the season when order in the Cardinals' bullpen was finally coming into focus. Despite the success that Boggs and Motte had individually in their roles, the team had suffered all season from problems in the sixth and seventh innings. A trade at the end of July, which brought in Edward Mujica from Miami, filled that void, solidifying Boggs's role of being called on almost exclusively to pitch the eighth inning when the Cardinals had a lead.

Boggs gave up a big home run to Erik Kratz of the Philadelphia Phillies four days after the Scutaro homer, but that was followed by another string of thirteen consecutive scoreless appearances. It was all part of a year that Boggs knew was possible but wondered, based on his experiences from 2011, if it would really happen. The fact that he was able to go through it with so many close friends, and fellow Christians, made it even more enjoyable.

"It's a blessing to be on this team," Boggs said. "It's easy for me when I go home in the off-season to have a commitment to my faith because there are so many people around me who are committed as well. It's the same here, because there are so many guys on this team who are truly committed. It makes it a lot easier when you have guys you know you can trust, guys you can go to, who help strengthen you. It's been amazing."

THIRTEEN

JASON MOTTE

For God so loved the world, that he gave his only begotten Son, that whosoever believeth in him should not perish, but have everlasting life.

—**John 3:16** KJV

As Jason Motte drove home from Busch Stadium on the night of August 16, he picked up his cell phone to call his wife, Caitlin, who he knew was out of town. Motte had just endured a bad night at the office, the first time in more than two years that he had allowed two home runs in a game. Just two outs away from an important win, with a key series against the Pittsburgh Pirates beginning the next night, the back-to-back homers by Paul Goldschmidt and Chris Young had turned a would-be 1–0 win for the Cardinals into a 2–1 loss to the Arizona Diamondbacks.

Even though Motte has the selective short-term memory necessary to be a topflight closer, it was comforting for him to talk to his wife after a disappointing outcome. Motte hung up the phone as he pulled into his driveway, expecting to go inside and try to watch television before finally going to bed. It was at that moment that Caitlin, who had not told her husband on the phone that she had come home a day earlier than expected, opened the garage door.

"Perfect," Motte said.

As he relaxed an hour or so later, logging on to Twitter to see what people were saying, that word came up again.

One Cardinals fan had sent Motte a tweet that read, "No one is perfect," trying to reassure him.

Motte wrote back, "One person was and bc [sic] of him I have peace."

Another fan, Kyle Thompson—a contestant at the MLB Fan Cave in New York—followed that conversation with a tweet back to Motte that included the Bible verse James 1:12, a verse tailor-made for a major league closer: "Blessed is the man who remains steadfast under trial, for when he has stood the test he will receive the crown of life, which God has promised to those who love him" (ESV).

Motte's final tweet of the night read, "Not my first, probably won't be my last. Learn from the mistakes, correct them, and go get 'em next time. #blessed."

Motte knows that, despite moments like what happened in that two-pitch sequence, he is indeed blessed to be playing major league baseball, and he never wants to forget that.

"There are things I find funny now, especially what people say on Twitter," Motte said. "People will write how terrible you are. I'm like, 'Man, I go out there and give it everything I have. It may not be a good day; it may be a bad day.'

"When I wrote back to the one guy that one person was perfect, and that's why I have peace, that's exactly the way I look at stuff like that. You look at the big picture and realize it's a game."

Motte enjoyed far more success than failure in 2012, becoming only the fourth pitcher in franchise history to record forty or more saves in a season. With forty-two saves, he tied for the league lead and became the first Cardinals pitcher ever to record all of the team's saves in a season. If Motte ever forgets how blessed he was to have a season such as 2012—or 2011, when he was on the mound to record the final out in game seven of the World Series—all Motte has to do is think back to a much more sobering conversation, which happened in a manager's office in Clearwater, Florida, in 2006.

The Cardinals drafted Motte in the nineteenth round in 2003, as a catcher out of Iona College. He struggled offensively in the minors before having one of the best days of his minor league career in a game for Double-A Springfield, Missouri.

"I had gone up there a couple of days earlier, but I didn't play until the last day I was there, and then I went 3-for-3 and threw out a couple of guys trying to steal," Motte said. "Chris Maloney [now the Cardinals' first-base coach] was the manager, and he called me into the office and said he had never had to do something like this before, send somebody down after a day like that."

That wasn't the news Motte wanted to hear. It was nothing, however, compared with the shocking news he got the following day when he joined the Class A Palm Beach, Florida, team. Several of the organization's coaches and roving instructors were there that day, and the message became pretty clear—they did not believe Motte had a future as a catcher, primarily because of his poor hitting, but they had another idea. They wanted Motte to try to become a pitcher.

"That tested my faith a lot," Motte said. "I had caught since I was eight years old. The only time I had pitched was when I was about twelve, just for a couple of innings. That was really it. I had caught my whole life, and it was the only thing I knew. They said, 'Now you are going to pitch.'"

After that message sank in for a couple of minutes, Motte knew he really didn't have any choice but to say yes. Otherwise, he would almost certainly be released and have to try to hook on with another organization or give up his dream of playing in the major leagues.

"Before we gave him his release, we decided to put him out on the mound and see what happened," said Mark DeJohn, who became Motte's first manager as a pitcher, in State College, Pennsylvania.

So a few weeks before his twenty-fourth birthday, Motte became a pitcher.

"It took me a day or so, but I finally was like, 'All right,'" Motte said. "God's got a plan, and He's got a reason He's doing this. I don't know what it is right now. Maybe I'm going to go out and play a couple of years and something is going to happen. Maybe I'm going to meet someone, or I don't know what. My mind-set honestly was, 'God has a plan, and I'm going to give it everything I've got and use the ability He gave me every single day.'"

Motte had no idea how pitching would work out. There were days when he thought it was not going well, and he wondered what he would have to do to go back to college and complete his degree and go find a teaching and coaching job. Other days went better and he thought maybe, just maybe, he had a chance.

"If God's plan had been for me to become a teacher and coach, that's what I would have done, and I would have been fine with that," Motte said.

As Motte started learning how to pitch, he realized that there really is not another position on the baseball field that is more of a testament to God's will.

"It's all kind of out of our hands when you look at it," Motte said. "But once I let the ball go, figuratively and literally, it is out of my hands. I can make a perfect pitch and the hitter smashes it. I can throw it right down the middle on an 0–2 pitch and the guy takes it for strike three."

Motte's education as a pitcher began in the extended spring

training program, and then he moved to the short-season team in State College.

"At the time I really had to kind of rely on faith," he said. "I was still single at the time, but I knew I had someone to talk to, regardless of the situation. I had Him. I knew He was going to get me through this, whether I was pitching or if I was going home. He's going to be there regardless. He has a plan for me, and I never would have believed when they turned me into a pitcher all the things that would happen to me."

The only thing Motte asked the Cardinals for in making the transition was to give him a chance, not to automatically give up on him if he struggled in his early outings. The Cardinals agreed they would not make any instant decisions. To this day, he remembers the first official game he pitched, in Williamsport, Pennsylvania.

"I just went out there and told myself to give it everything I had to every batter, just like it would be my last," he said.

Motte knew throwing fast would not be a problem. He had always had the best arm on his team as a youngster growing up, even if he was the catcher.

"I was just always able to throw," he said. "It was a God-given ability."

After showing promise at the extended spring training program, Motte was sent to State College, with great results for somebody making his professional debut as a pitcher. In 21 games, Motte worked 26 innings, struck out 25 batters, and issued only 4 walks. That earned him a promotion to Quad Cities, a full-season Class A team, to finish the season. There, he had 13 strikeouts and 3 walks in 12 innings.

By the start of the 2007 season, Motte was in Palm Beach, and after only nine games, in which he allowed only one earned run in ten innings, Motte was on the move again, this time to Double-A

Springfield. The totals again were impressive: 63 strikeouts in 49 innings, with a 2.20 ERA.

The 2008 season was special for Motte, as he found himself at Triple-A Memphis, one level below the major leagues. He found something else that summer too—Caitlin, who would later become his wife.

"She was at a game with some friends, and I saw her, and then I saw her again later and we started talking," Motte said. "From the get-go it just kind of clicked, and we both knew."

The complication was that Caitlin had just taken a job working with the women's basketball program at the University of Southern Mississippi, and she was moving away from Memphis.

"Neither of us knew how it was going to work out, but we both had faith," Motte said. "She was [at Southern Mississippi] for a year, and then came back and we got married."

Motte's career was going as well as his private life. When the major league rosters expanded for the final month of the season, Motte found himself in St. Louis, where he pitched in twelve games. He earned his first major league save and, in 11 innings, recorded 16 strikeouts and allowed only 3 walks, posting a 0.82 ERA.

During spring training in 2009, manager Tony La Russa made Motte the team's new closer, and on opening day handed him the ball for the ninth inning, entrusting him to protect a 4–2 lead over the Pittsburgh Pirates.

Motte allowed a leadoff double, but then got two quick outs. Before he could record the third out, he allowed a single, followed by a double; then he hit a batter and allowed another double. By that time four runs had scored, and the Pirates were headed to a 6–4 victory.

"Izzy [Jason Isringhausen] called me and Frankie [Ryan Franklin] talked to me," Motte said. "They both said, 'It's your first, but it won't be your last.' I know people thought I was terrible whether they said it or not. I was still able to see the bigger picture."

Motte knew it was not God's fault that he had blown the save and the Cardinals had lost the game. While, understandably, he was not happy, he did not blame God for what happened.

"It's easy to think sometimes that because I helped a lady across the street, or went to the Rainbows for Kids All-Star game, that God owes me to go 3-for-3 today or throw a shutout inning," Motte said. "But if I start thinking like that, what happens if I do something nice and then go 0-for-3 or give up a four-spot? Is it God's fault? It's not God's fault.

"Everyone has sinned and falls short of the glory of God. We are not going to be perfect. I could think, *I yelled at this guy today and that's why I gave up three runs.* Seeing the bigger picture is the reality of knowing that God isn't worried about whether the Cardinals won today. All I can do is try to get the next guy out no matter what has happened before. That's just the way I look at it."

Motte grew up in a Southern Baptist home. His family moved a lot when he was young but always tried to find a church home; if they couldn't find one, they had a service at home. Religion has always been a daily part of Motte's life.

As often happens with young adults, Motte got a little away from religion during his college years. His faith quickly came back to him, however, once he started playing professional baseball and has only gotten stronger since he reached the major leagues.

"Around here there are people who hold you accountable," Motte said. "We have a good group of Christian guys in here. It kind of makes you look at things a little differently. Sometimes people in this game, or just in life in general, think a rule doesn't apply to them. Anything can happen. When your time is up, it's up. When you think like that, it makes you reevaluate your life, and make sure that you are doing the right thing and doing things the right way."

After suffering that blown save on opening day in 2009, Motte pitched in sixty-eight more games that season, but none of them came in a save situation. He did not pick up his second career save until April 27, 2010. He pitched almost exclusively in a setup role all season, and that was what he was doing again through the first few months of the 2011 season.

From August 28, 2011, on, however, Motte found himself pitching in the ninth inning when the Cardinals had a lead—even though La Russa refused to call him the team's closer. He saved nine games in the Cardinals' final twenty-eight games of the season as they completed an unprecedented comeback to qualify for the postseason.

Motte came through then as well, earning five saves in the postseason, including getting the final out in game seven, which secured the Cardinals' eleventh World Series championship.

One of the moments that flashed through his mind during the postgame celebration was of being in that small manager's office in Clearwater when he was told the Cardinals were going to release him unless he wanted to try to become a pitcher.

"From that moment, to thinking I would be on the mound getting the last out of the World Series, would never have crossed my mind," he said.

Motte knows who to thank for his success—the same God he thanks for allowing him to have more success as a closer in 2012, reaching that forty-save plateau. Having so many strong Christians around to share his success has made it all that much better for Motte.

"I don't know how else to explain it except that he gets it," Motte said about his manager, Matheny. "He understands what he's doing here, and he understands his job here, to put a team on the field and win ball games. But he understands the bigger picture too.

"I will get a text message from him after a good game or a bad game. 'Hey, keep your head up, you're doing a great job.' The guys in this clubhouse are the same way. If somebody has a bad day, he's not ripping the TV off the wall or going crazy, or going home and breaking something or kicking the dog. That's the great thing about our situation here—it's not just baseball accountability.

"Every person in this clubhouse knows whenever anyone is on the field, they are giving it everything they have. And after the game, seven or eight guys will go out together to get something to eat. While we're there, we might get into a discussion about the Bible. We always get together on the road for Bible study. Everybody on this team knows somebody has his back."

Motte was not always as comfortable talking openly about his strong faith, but the more he has been around the other players on the Cardinals, and the more success he has had, the more comfortable he has become with speaking out. It is not unusual for him and other relief pitchers to get in a religious discussion, or to bring up something they discussed in Bible study, while sitting in the bullpen during the early innings of a game.

"The more you're around guys, the more comfortable you get," Motte said. "I kind of feel better about opening up to some of the older guys. When young guys come up, you try to make them feel comfortable and [tell them] that it's okay to talk about your faith. There is no stigma attached to it."

As one of the more veteran players in the Cardinals' bullpen in 2012, it also fell to Motte to talk with some of the young relievers about the proper way to approach their jobs—and the proper way to keep it all in perspective. One of the questions he gets most often comes after a night like that game in August when the Diamondbacks hit the two homers. It didn't matter that it was the first time he had blown a save in two months—after thirteen saves and a win between those two games—all that is forgotten by fans and the media in the immediate aftermath of the game.

"Guys ask me, 'How do you forget about it?'" Motte said. "Honestly, my faith helps a lot. One of my favorite Bible verses is John 3:16, and it is one of those verses that lets you know that no matter what happens, He is there for you. That's how I feel after I pitch, no matter if it's a good night or a bad night.

"Just because a guy is religious doesn't mean he can't have a bad game. But it can't control your life. That night, as I left, I ran into Trevor Rosenthal's wife in the hallway and we had some small talk. She told Trevor later that she thought that was amazing, and she didn't know how I could do that.

"When I walk out of the locker room, honestly that is the last time I think about what happened. I have to do it when the media wants to talk about it, but when they leave, it's over."

Luckily for Motte, he had far more good days than bad days during the 2012 season. After a five-save week in August, he became the first relief pitcher to be named Player of the Week in the National League in more than two years.

"On good days and bad days both, I am just so blessed to be here, and blessed to have the opportunity to play baseball," Motte said.

FOURTEEN

MATT HOLLIDAY

Where were you when I laid the earth's foundation? Tell me, if you understand.

—Job 38:4 NIV

The Cardinals were at a crossroads when September began. They had lost four games in a row in the middle of a critical ten-game road trip, having been outscored 32–1, as they tried to remain alive for a possible postseason berth.

Halfway through a four-game series in Washington, the Cardinals were coming off a 10–0 rout by the Nationals. Two days earlier they had lost starting shortstop Rafael Furcal for the season because of an elbow injury. This day did not begin any better, as the Nationals jumped on Kyle Lohse for four runs in the first inning.

Some players might have started to panic or think that maybe the final month of the season was simply not going to go the Cardinals' way. Anybody on the team's bench who thought that way probably would have been advised to stay away from Matt Holliday.

"He might not be the loudest guy all the time, but when he talks, people listen," said teammate Adam Wainwright.

Holliday also doesn't always use his mouth when he talks. Sometimes he uses his bat.

His twenty-fifth home run of the year, a two-run shot in the third inning, contributed to a Cardinals comeback that produced a 10–9 victory and saved the team from a potentially devastating loss. Nobody knew at the time, of course, what that singular victory could mean as the final month of the season unfolded, but the players inside the Cardinals' locker room were not surprised that Holliday was right in the middle of the comeback. Though there are players on the team who grab more headlines, or whip out more quotable phrases, there is no player on the Cardinals more respected or admired by his teammates than Holliday.

"I think Matt is misunderstood a lot," said teammate Kyle McClellan. "He doesn't want to be out in front very often, but he has got a huge heart and is very much a leader. He is not a guy who is going to jump in front of a camera and tell everybody about it."

Holliday is the same way when it comes to talking about his faith. He knows that Wainwright and Lance Berkman are much more outgoing and vocal, and he is fine with letting them capture the limelight.

"I think it's more about the type of people we are," Holliday said. "I like to think my passion for Jesus is equal to theirs, but Lance is probably the most outgoing guy I know and Adam also. I don't consider myself shy but I'm not a big talker."

Yet it is in Holliday's room where many of the players gather on the road, to hang out, play video games, or just talk. Many of the team's younger or more inexperienced players, such as David Freese, have called upon him for advice and counseling over the years, and Holliday has been happy to provide that service.

"Matt has a great gift of being a receiver, a shepherd," Wainwright said. "He is very welcoming. Guys want to hang out with him and go to his room and just be with him. Matt has that infectious personality."

Added Freese, "Matt likes to love on people. He doesn't push the Word. Other guys in this clubhouse are like that too, and that isn't wrong. That's just the way they go about it."

It really is the only way that Holliday knows, because it was the way he was taught. The son of a college baseball coach, he has always preached the importance of team, the knowledge that baseball is not, never has been, and never will be a one-man sport.

"It's very important to me that we have a great corps of guys here who are trying to learn and grow," Holliday said. "We kind of count on each other because we are all in this together. Lance, Adam, and I are kind of the leaders, but we are all trying to grow.

"Obviously, being a good player is very important to me, but being a friend and somebody guys can talk to is really my goal. The relationship aspect of baseball is really what transcends beyond your career. Those are the things the Bible talks about, relationships and loving [one another] as brothers. That is my hope and prayer, that I can be somebody others can easily talk to."

Holliday believes that way because he was once the younger player, the unproven talent seeking out advice and help from the older veterans and coaches on his team.

Holliday was both a high school football star and a baseball star in Stillwater, Oklahoma, a quarterback who was ranked among the top prospects in the country, as well as a hard-hitting third baseman who most scouts projected as a first-round talent. Because his father, Tom, was the head baseball coach at Oklahoma State, he had grown up around that environment. Whenever his dad had players—such as former Oklahoma State star and major leaguer Robin Ventura, now the manager of the Chicago White Sox—visiting his house, the younger Holliday would often eavesdrop on their conversations.

Holliday loved both sports, and wanted to continue to play both, with good reason. As a junior quarterback, he set a state record in Oklahoma, passing for thirty-five touchdowns. As a senior, he led Stillwater to a 43–42 victory over rival Tulsa Union after his team trailed 42–21 with a little more than six minutes remaining. He threw for 375 yards and 4 touchdowns in that game, part of the 2,310 yards and 21 touchdowns he accumulated as a senior, when he was named to the Parade All-American football team.

He finished his high school football career with 6,200 yards passing and 68 touchdowns in three seasons, a school record. He could throw a football 70 yards in the air, and former coach Jimmy Johnson told Holliday's father his son was a "couldn't miss" NFL prospect. Holliday liked the idea of playing for his father with the Oklahoma State baseball team, as his older brother Josh had done, but the offers of football scholarships from schools such as Florida State, Penn State, and UCLA were enticing. Finally, he made up his mind and told a crowd of about two hundred people at his high school in December 1997 what he was going to do.

"I've decided to go to Florida State," the 6-foot-4, 215-pound Holliday deadpanned. He was joking, he told the crowd, and then said he was going to his hometown Cowboys.

Holliday thought his future was settled—until baseball season came around the next spring and Holliday put together a year that made scouts start talking about big bonuses and a high draft spot.

Some teams, however, were worried because of Holliday's football commitment. They did not want to pick him with a high selection, then have him turn down the offer and go off to play both sports in college.

"I'm a Cowboy," Holliday said. "I have been since I was born. I really did look at other schools, but this is where I want to be."

As many as six baseball teams, however, told Holliday's father they were prepared to take his son in the first round. They knew it would cost more money to buy him out of the football scholarship, but it was a commitment their organizations were willing to make. He worked out privately for at least fifteen teams, including the Pirates, who flew him to Pittsburgh for a workout at Three Rivers Stadium.

On the day of the draft, Holliday was eager to see what happened. Then the first round came and went without his name being called. So did the second round, then the third. It wasn't until the seventh round, with the 210th overall selection, that Holliday was selected by the Colorado Rockies.

After getting over his initial disappointment, Holliday met with a scout for the Rockies—his uncle Dave—and began to seriously consider how much he wanted to play professional baseball. Was the team's offer enough to convince him to give up not only playing college football but also playing baseball for his father? In the end, he decided the answer was yes, and he signed with the Rockies. He was assigned to the rookie league team in Arizona, said good-bye to his parents, and started out on a new journey.

There were times when he was in the minors, especially on those days when he struggled, or when he got a glimpse of packed college football stadiums around the country, that Holliday wondered if he had made the right choice. He had grown up in a Christian environment, even though the Holliday family did not go to church much because of his father's baseball commitment. It was while he was playing in the minors, and facing all the challenges a young adult faces no matter what walk of life he is in, that Holliday started to turn more to God and ask for His help in guiding his life.

"When you sign out of high school you don't really have those college years. The minor leagues sort of turn into your growing-up years," Holliday said. "A lot of people use college for that, and kind of figuring out who you are as a person and where your life is going, where your path in life is going to take you."

Sometimes, Holliday wasn't sure of the answer.

"I had a lot of sleepless nights because of the struggles and difficulties in the minors, figuring out how to play this game," he said. "There was a lot of growth going on. In those years between eighteen and twenty-three you make a lot of mistakes figuring out who you are."

One of the challenges Holliday was still dealing with was college football coaches, who remembered him as the strapping young high school quarterback and were hoping—after one long minor league bus ride or a frustrating night in a dimly lit ballpark with only a few hundred people watching—that he would change his mind and decide to come back and play football for their university.

Holliday fought off those urges and stuck with baseball.

In the 2000 season, playing for the Class A Salem Avalanche in Virginia, Holliday met an older player named Jay Jones. Jones was twenty-five then, five years older than Holliday, and though he never made it above Double-A in five minor league seasons, he quickly became a valuable mentor for Holliday.

"I had a couple of guys who became like mentors to me, including Jones," Holliday said. "I just saw something different in them and the way they lived their lives, the way they interacted with their family and teammates. It was very appealing."

Two years later, Holliday was at Double-A Carolina when he met Seth Taylor, who became another mentor. Taylor, like Jones, played seven years in the minors without advancing past Double-A, but he had an influence on Holliday that Holliday still remembers years later.

"Just talking to those guys, and going to Bible studies and

chapel, made a difference in my life," Holliday said. "I always felt I had a heart for God, but I had to learn a lot about really committing yourself to Jesus. It was a gradual process. I also had a lot of pastors along the way that the Lord placed in my life.

"It has become very clear as you look back you can see the dots are connected and you realize things don't just happen by chance. I had a lot of people in my life who have spoken to me and taught me a lot, giving me lots of insight."

Holliday's journey through the minor leagues took six years before he reached the majors with the Rockies in 2004, when he was called up from Triple-A because Preston Wilson suffered a knee injury. He made his major league debut in the tenth game of the season, on April 16—in St. Louis, of all places, where the man who would turn out to be his manager in 2012, Mike Matheny, was the starting catcher for the Cardinals. Holliday went 0-for-3, grounding into one double play after drawing a walk in his first plate appearance.

Holliday went on to have a solid rookie season, and by the time he had played two years with the Rockies, was considered one of the best young players in the game. He was still watching and learning, as he had done in the minor leagues. Two veterans whom he tried to emulate were Todd Greene and Todd Helton.

"We had a chaplain there, Bill Rader, who has been a friend of mine for a long time," Holliday said. "Matt Herges was another guy who was there. Watching him live out his faith was a big encouragement to me. The Bible talks a lot about community and relationship. The game is fun, but those things are eternal."

As Holliday has transitioned through his career, he has experienced many trials and challenges. He went from a high of helping Colorado win the National League pennant in 2007, when he led the league with 216 hits, 50 doubles, 137 RBI, and a .340 average, to the sad reality that, financially, the Rockies were not going to be able to afford to sign him to a new contract.

One person who watched how Holliday handled that period in his life and career was Clint Hurdle, who had been his manager with the Rockies and had noticed Holliday as he grew from that shy, young player into one of the best in the game.

"He grew up in front of my eyes, and I loved watching it," Hurdle said. "As a Double-A player he was doing good, and you thought he might be okay, he might be good, to where he got in the big leagues, where I saw what challenged him.

"I really thought he was the MVP in 2007. That was a special year for him, and he stayed humble. We had a challenging situation one time, during a game in Arizona. Matt made a base-running mistake, and somebody got thrown out and we didn't score a run.

"The next day I called him in the office and told him he wasn't playing. It was a hustle factor. He said, 'Clint, I was wrong.' I told him it was just something we had to do, and to be on the bench and be ready. Veteran players came up to me and told me we were risking losing this guy and not to do it, but my feeling was that if we lost him over that, we never had him.

"He told me, 'I promise I will never do it again.' I said, 'Matt, I know you won't. But I want to make sure twenty-four other guys don't either.' He handled it professionally, and we went on from there. We didn't lose him. He should have been the MVP.

"I watched him become a father. He earned the nickname Big Daddy. I watched him grow and evolve."

The most challenging point in his career, and perhaps to his faith, came when Holliday was traded to Oakland prior to the 2009 season.

"We were comfortable in Colorado," Holliday said. "We had a home there. But it got to the point where we talked about it and prayed about it and it just didn't feel right. When I was traded to

Oakland it was tough. We knew it probably was going to be a transition year. It's a tough stadium and a tough place to play, but it was good for me, and good for us as a family."

Holliday struggled with the Oakland Athletics, having to face American League pitchers and adjust to playing in different ballparks, getting to know new teammates and adapting to living in a different city—a city he knew he was not going to be in when he became a free agent at the end of the season.

Luckily for Holliday, that period in his life lasted for only four months before he was traded to the Cardinals. He was happy in his new city, and happy to be back in the National League. It wasn't long, however, before Holliday had another major test of his faith. As a free agent, he was eligible to sign with any team, and he chose to come back to the Cardinals with a seven-year deal, the largest financial agreement in franchise history.

That put pressure on Holliday, including from himself, to show he was worthy of that kind of commitment from the team.

"There were high expectations from a lot of people, including myself, mostly because of the money part of it," Holliday said. "But I learned during that period that if everything was easy you wouldn't rely on the Lord. You wouldn't grow and you would count on yourself. A lot of life is trials and how you deal with them, and relying on Him to make you a path. You want to always be running toward God and not running away from Him. You have to understand that there is learning to be had.

"Sometimes it's tough; I'm not going to lie. But a lot of people have had a lot tougher circumstances in their lives than I have had. I can't imagine how some of the people I know, dealing with cancer or sick children, do it. We do a lot of work at Cardinal Glennon Children's Medical Center, and you see how strong the faith is in those families and those kids. I think one of the beauties of the Lord is that He provides strength in times of weakness."

What impressed Clint Hurdle from a distance was how Holliday met and dealt with those challenges and came away from them stronger and more focused, not only about his career but about his life and his faith.

"He found a balance, and that's significant," Hurdle said. "I'm proud of him, I'm happy for him, and I'm happy to know him. I tell him that every time I see him and tell him to 'Remember who you are and what you are. You are special.'"

As Holliday has grown into becoming one of the veterans on the Cardinals and a team leader, he has realized the importance of becoming more outspoken about his faith and trying to help younger players struggling not only to find their place in baseball but also in their walks with God.

"Being grateful and humbled by the opportunities we have is important," Holliday said. "Sometimes young players don't understand that. Our job as players who have been around for a while is to make sure they do understand. That gets back to the relationship part of the game. When you get together on the road, those are the times you feel the most fulfilled—spending time with guys and talking about things that are eternal.

"I think I am growing into that role. I come from a point of being very shy about my faith, as far as not knowing very much about the Bible, to continuing to try to learn more. My relationship with the Lord has grown to where I feel much more comfortable talking about my faith when I get the opportunity to talk to teammates and other people. I have things to say that I think the Lord would want me to say. I've grown a lot but I still have a lot of growing to do."

One of the ways Holliday tried to help younger players even before the 2012 season began was to invite several of the organization's top prospects to St. Louis, at his expense, for five days. He wanted them to see Busch Stadium and the city and get to know some of the other players on the major league roster.

"When I was a young player, I had a chance to go to a rookie development camp and got to be in the city, the clubhouse, and work out in the stadium," Holliday said. "That made it more comfortable when I did get a chance to play in the majors. For some of these guys now, when they get here it will not be their first time in the stadium and not the first time around some of these people.

"The Lord has blessed me with some resources to do that for guys. I thought it was a good idea if I could lend a helping hand. I worked with Mo [general manager John Mozeliak] about it beforehand about which guys to invite."

With Mozeliak's help, Holliday invited prospects Kolten Wong, Matt Adams, Ryan Jackson, and Charlie Tilson to St. Louis for the all-expenses-paid week. When Wong received the text message, he first thought it was a joke coming from one of his friends. He later realized Holliday was sincere, and he and the other invited guests came to St. Louis for the week, which even included having dinner several times at Holliday's home. Holliday plans to do it every season he remains with the Cardinals.

"We'll look for guys who are on the cusp of being here," he said. "That's probably how I will do it."

It is just one more way Holliday is trying to give back to the Cardinals, and to the game that has blessed him so well.

"I don't think it's by chance that I ended up here and have an opportunity to learn and grow from these guys," he said. "The sanctification part of being a Christian is a daily battle. We all struggle with sin every day; it's part of the battle of living in the world. We live for things that are eternal. Being in a community like this helps us battle those things.

"I've got young kids to raise and a wife to lead. I've got plenty on my plate. I'd like to continue to get better at baseball, but, Lord willing, I've got a lot of time after baseball with a wife and three kids, and the Bible tells me I have a huge role in their lives."

The 2012 season was good for Holliday, who bounced back from an injury-filled 2011 when he played in only 124 games. Holliday missed only 5 of the Cardinals' games in 2012 and hit .295 with 27 homers and 102 RBI, his fifth season with 100 or more RBI. Holliday reached that milestone with a two-run single on September 24 in Houston.

The combination of on-field success with his off-field involvement in charity and community events earned Holliday the Cardinals' nomination for the annual Roberto Clemente award, presented each year by Major League Baseball to the player who best represents the game of baseball through positive contributions on and off the field. The winner for 2012 was Clayton Kershaw of the Dodgers.

Since moving to St. Louis, Holliday and his wife, Leslee, have been involved with the Make-A-Wish Foundation and Cardinal Glennon Children's Medical Center, and in 2012, they stepped in to serve as the honorary chairmen of the Albert Pujols Family Foundation golf tournament to benefit Down syndrome research and programs.

Holliday, whose contract with the Cardinals runs through 2017, seldom needs a reminder that his life is about more than baseball, but if he does, all he has to do is look at his left arm.

"It's just a daily reminder to me," Holliday said of having his favorite Bible verse, Job 38:4, tattooed onto his arm. "A lot of times we as people want to be our own gods and dictate what goes on in our lives, and it's a reminder to me that says He's God and He created this earth and we're not. It's something I like to go back to."

FIFTEEN

JAKE WESTBROOK

Have I not commanded you? Be strong and of good courage; do
not be afraid, nor be dismayed, for the LORD your God is with you
wherever you go.

—Joshua 1:9 NKJV

There were many reasons why Jake Westbrook was in a good
mood as he walked to the mound to start the Cardinals' game on
September 8 against the Milwaukee Brewers.

The team was in playoff contention with three weeks left in
the season. A week earlier, Westbrook had agreed to a new contract with the Cardinals, keeping him in St. Louis for the 2013
season instead of forcing him to test the free agent market and
possibly have to leave a team and town where he really wanted
to stay.

A win over the Brewers also would bring his career victory
total to ninety-nine, one away from a goal he had set for himself a
couple of years earlier of one hundred career victories. Westbrook
has pitched long enough, however, to realize that as good as things
may seem, they can change in a hurry. On this night, it took five
innings.

While pitching to Aramis Ramirez in the fifth inning, Westbrook suffered a pulled muscle in his oblique. He knew it when it happened, and it was a disappointed Westbrook who walked off the mound after the inning. Because he had suffered the injury twice earlier in his career, Westbrook knew it probably was going to be serious enough to keep him from pitching for the rest of the season, and that was exactly what happened.

"It's a tough time," he said a few days later. "You have to deal with the disappointment of not being able to participate when you want to be out there helping the team. An injury is disappointing and is something that tests your faith. It really makes you rely on God."

Unfortunately for Westbrook, this was not the first time he found himself out of action because of an injury. He had spent seven different stints on the disabled list during his first nine years in the major leagues, giving him plenty of experience with how to deal with being hurt. It is experience Westbrook really has never enjoyed, but one he acknowledges has a silver lining.

"It's a time to kind of reflect and realize that you are not in control," Westbrook said. "God is in control, and He has me in this position for a reason. It's up to me to figure out why this is happening. I have to reflect on what He wants from me and my life."

The injury was a blow to Westbrook because, up until that happened, he had been enjoying a solid season, coming back from the disappointment of being left off the roster for the 2011 National League Championship Series as the Cardinals were making a run toward the World Series.

"You learn something from every situation," Westbrook said. "I was not pitching as well then as I would have liked, but it also allowed me to trust more in Him, and taught me to keep a good attitude and do whatever needed to be done for the team. You have to keep the attitude of doing whatever it takes."

Westbrook was, in fact, added to the roster for the World Series and turned out to be the winning pitcher coming out of the bullpen in game six, which will be remembered throughout history as one of the greatest World Series games ever played—a night the Cardinals were down to their last strike twice before rallying to win.

"God rewarded me and the team," Westbrook said. "It was a good opportunity for me to know that God has a plan for us and for me."

Ever since he was a young boy growing up in rural small-town Georgia, Westbrook thought God's plan for his life was for him to become a major league baseball player. He didn't know back then, however, how many challenges and obstacles God was going to place in front of him along the way.

"All the things that I have gone through in my career definitely have made me stronger and given me the opportunity to handle these situations a little better, mentally and spiritually," Westbrook said. "God's molding me, making me the man He wants me to be."

That molding began as Westbrook was growing up in Danielsville, Georgia, a town of about five hundred residents not far from Athens. Growing up in a Christian home and going to church on a regular basis gave Westbrook a solid foundation as his career began as an eighteen-year-old first-round draft pick of the Colorado Rockies, the twenty-first overall selection in 1996. Westbrook decided to sign with the Rockies instead of accepting a scholarship to play baseball at the University of Georgia. A few months later, away from home for the first time, Westbrook wasn't certain he had made the right choice.

"Going straight into pro baseball out of high school is not an easy life," Westbrook said, "especially spiritually, because of all the temptations that are out there. There are a lot of things that come with being a professional athlete. My faith really gave me the strength to get through it. I didn't have the comfort level of being around friends and family, and that made me rely on God.

"I used the time to focus on Him instead of other things. That was probably one of the hardest points of my career, going through that first year. It was a trying time. I really felt like if I could get through that year, I could really do this."

At that time, of course, Westbrook had no idea of what other challenges were looming ahead of him. Some of those came quickly, in the form of trades—Westbrook found himself traded three times, moving through four organizations before he celebrated his twenty-third birthday.

"I was the guy everybody wanted but nobody really wanted that much," Westbrook said. "It really helped me, as I went to whatever new team I was going to, that the main guy I had was God. I had to meet all of my new teammates, and get to know them, but God was always there with me, and that was comforting."

That's the reason Westbrook's favorite Bible verse is Joshua 1:9, because it reminds him that God is with him wherever he goes—even to Yankee Stadium, when Westbrook made his major league debut on June 17, 2000.

By that time, the twenty-two-year-old Westbrook already had been traded twice—by the Rockies to the Montreal Expos, and then by the Expos to the Yankees. After pitching just sixteen games in Triple-A, he found himself putting on a Yankee uniform as the team's starting pitcher against the Chicago White Sox. If that was not enough pressure in itself, add in the fact Westbrook was taking the place of Roger Clemens, who had gone on the disabled list.

The start did not go well. Pitching in front of more than fifty-four thousand fans, a population more than 108 times the total number of residents in his hometown, Westbrook failed to get through the second inning. Seven of the first eleven hitters he faced got hits, and Westbrook walked two more. After Magglio Ordóñez hit a three-run homer, manager Joe Torre mercifully took the ball from Westbrook.

The New York press, as might have been expected, was not kind to Westbrook, not caring about the small-town youngster's nerves or his feelings of being overwhelmed by the situation. The *Daily News* headline the next morning read, "Westbrook comes up, flames out." The *Post* headline was not much better: "Westbrook's no help for sinking ship."

Torre was more sympathetic. When the team was losing 17–4 the next night, he brought Westbrook into the game in relief. Westbrook pitched 2 1/3 scoreless innings, helping him somewhat forget his first trip to the mound. Four days later he made his second career start in about as unfriendly a place as a Yankee could be—Fenway Park in Boston, starting against the Red Sox. He fared slightly better than in his first start, this time getting eight outs before leaving the game with the Red Sox winning 4–2.

That week and those three games alone might have been enough to discourage some pitchers who did not have Westbrook's strong foundation. It was still concerning to him, but he didn't have much time to think about it before he was called into Torre's office. Thinking the news might be that he was being sent back to the minor leagues, Westbrook instead got a much stronger jolt—he had been traded again, this time to the Cleveland Indians as part of a package that brought David Justice to the Yankees.

"It was all part of growing and getting better," Westbrook said. "You have to learn from the situations that you are put in. My first couple of starts early on, I definitely learned from those things. That made me a stronger person and a stronger player."

After splitting time between Triple-A and the majors the next two seasons, Westbrook found himself back in the majors by 2004, becoming part of a young rotation in Cleveland that included a couple of other pitchers trying to establish themselves on their way to standout careers—CC Sabathia and Cliff Lee.

Westbrook won a combined forty-four games between 2004 and 2006 and helped Cleveland reach game seven of the American League Championship Series against the Boston Red Sox in 2007. He got the ball to start that game, once again in Fenway Park, his second start of the series. He worked six innings in the elimination game, giving up single runs in the first three innings, and trailed 3–2 when he left the game, which the Red Sox went on to win 11–2.

Players who come that close to the World Series often wonder if they will ever get that chance again, and for Westbrook, that was a very real concern when he experienced the first serious injury of his career in 2008.

Two months into the season, Westbrook's right elbow was hurting so badly he could not pick up a baseball. A trip to the doctor's office revealed that he needed Tommy John surgery. The recovery and rehab would keep him off the mound for most of the next twenty-one months—more time, Westbrook realized along the way, when his faith in God would be tested and ultimately strengthened. He knew the statistics: a sizeable majority of pitchers who undergo the surgery are able to come back and pitch as well, if not better, than they did before they were hurt. Still, the fact remains that some pitchers never come back.

"You always have those thoughts in your mind," Westbrook said. "You try to stay away from them and be as positive as you can. The scariest part was not knowing how I was going to be able to bounce back at age thirty-two.

"Having faith in God kind of gives you peace that if it happens, it happens. If it doesn't, then that's what God wants from me. I'm really blessed to do what I've always wanted to do, and that's compete and play this game for a living."

During his rehab and recovery, Westbrook realized that God was with him every step of the way. God had not abandoned him because he was not able to pitch. That was when he realized that because God was there for him, he needed to be there for God.

"I think God works in your life more so at times when things are not going well or not going your way," he said. "It's easy to be gung ho for God when things are going great. At other times it's just God making you stronger when He puts you in situations when things aren't going great. It kind of shapes you as a man and allows you to grow."

Westbrook was able to come back from the surgery. He made twenty-one starts for the Indians in the first half of the 2010 season, then found himself asking again for God's help. Having spent almost ten years in the Cleveland organization, and more than seven years in the major leagues, he was very comfortable there. Maybe, he realized, God thought he was too comfortable, something that changed when Westbrook was traded to the Cardinals, a team where the only player he knew and had played with in the past, Ryan Ludwick, was one of the players whom he was traded for in the three-way deal with the San Diego Padres.

Although he worried about how he would be able to fit in and adjust to life as a Cardinal, Westbrook soon learned it was something God had taken care of for him. Immediately upon joining the Cardinals, Westbrook found himself surrounded by a group of strong Christians, a pleasant by-product of the trade.

"This is the most spiritual group of guys on a team I have ever been on," Westbrook said. "These are guys you can rely on. When you spend time with them, you know you are in a good spot and a good situation, and there are a lot of things you don't have to worry about. It makes it easier to have those guys to fall back on, guys who have that accountability.

"That was one of the huge reasons why I wanted to come

back here for next year [2013]. The atmosphere of the team is just so great. There are so many guys when we get together for Bible studies and things like that, that if it so happens a couple of guys can't make it, we still have a good group. That wouldn't be the case on other teams. Here guys are always in the Word and talking about it every day. It just gives you a better feeling when you come to the park."

Being on the Cardinals, Westbrook said, has helped him realize that as much as he loves playing baseball and wants to succeed, there is ultimately a more important goal for him and everybody else.

"I know our ultimate purpose is not baseball, it's glorifying Him," Westbrook said. "Here it is about playing the game the right way, and knowing where our focus is.

"It was always a dream of mine to do this, and I know how blessed I have been that He gave me the opportunities and blessings that I have. I have to keep that mind-set, and not get too caught up in *me* doing it. I want to always keep that humble attitude and know how much He has blessed me to be able to fulfill this dream. When you remember that it keeps you grounded and not full of yourself."

Because of that attitude, Westbrook always has been able to understand and deal with frustrations caused by injuries or other situations that have kept him from pitching. There always is a reason, he said, and at some point God usually reveals it to him.

With his latest injury, Westbrook found the reason after the regular season was over, after the Cardinals had advanced to the playoffs. Had he been able to pitch and been on the active roster, he might not have been able to go back to his home in Georgia and be there when his wife, Heather, gave birth to their fourth child in October 2012.

It is a testament to Westbrook's faith that the youth who once pitched six no-hitters during his high school career at Madison County High School in Danielsville has turned into a professional baseball player who is still more comfortable living in his tiny hometown than anywhere else.

"It's not like I struck everybody out," he said of the no-hitters during his prep career. "It's a tiny, small town, but it's where I grew up and it's where I always want to be. There are a lot of great people there, and it's where my family's from. It's a place where I feel comfortable."

The same could be said about being on the Cardinals, where his latest injury has only delayed Westbrook's quest for his one-hundredth career victory, which he hopes will come early in the 2013 season.

"I don't really think about numbers and things like that," he said, "but it would be nice to get it. I want to stay in this game for as long as I can, but you never know what's going to happen."

Whatever happens, however, Westbrook will be ready for it.

SIXTEEN

CARLOS BELTRAN

I can do all things through Christ, because he gives me strength.

—**Philippians 4:13** NCV

One of the primary reasons Carlos Beltran signed with the Cardinals as a free agent before the 2012 season was a chance to play in the World Series.

It was about the only goal that had eluded Beltran through the first fourteen years of his major league career. He had come close twice, reaching the seventh game of the National League Championship Series with the Astros in 2004 and the Mets in 2006. Each time he had to watch the Cardinals celebrate winning the pennant, but the 2006 loss is an especially painful memory.

Beltran was at the plate with the bases loaded and two outs in the bottom of the ninth, the Mets trailing by two runs, 3–1. A base hit could easily have tied the game and sent it to extra innings. An extra-base hit would have won the pennant for the Mets. The Cardinals' rookie pitcher Adam Wainwright was on the mound. The first pitch was a changeup for a called strike one.

"We knew [Beltran] was a very patient hitter, but at the same time, we didn't want to throw a cookie up there where he could try to tee off," Wainwright said after the game.

His second pitch was a curveball, which Beltran fouled off for strike two, leaving him in an 0–2 hole.

As Beltran took a deep breath and steadied himself in the batter's box, Wainwright did the same on the mound—then delivered one of the best backdoor curveballs of his life. Beltran was frozen, and could only watch as umpire Tim Welke threw up his right hand for the game-ending strike three.

"Sometimes you have to live with good memories in this game, and sometimes you have to live with bad memories," Beltran said in the silence of the Mets' clubhouse that night. "Today was bad. I was trying to put the ball in play and just couldn't do anything with it. I tracked it all the way to the glove, and I was hoping the umpire called a ball or something. It was a strike. Game over."

Beltran struggled with that one at-bat, that one missed opportunity, knowing it would be remembered far longer than any of the forty-one homers he hit for the Mets that year in the regular season, or the three homers he had hit in the playoff series against the Cardinals, extending his record of postseason success.

The following day Beltran watched a replay of the at-bat, which lasted only slightly more than one minute. It was the same as he remembered it. Among all the messages of support Beltran received that day was one from Cali Magallanes, the chapel minister for the Mets.

Beltran replied, "It's okay, brother. God is in control."

While that pitch united Wainwright and Beltran forever in baseball history, the two didn't talk about that moment for more than five years. They met on the baseball diamond only once over that stretch, on July 27, 2010, when Beltran went 2-for-3 off Wainwright, now a starter, collecting a single and double as the Mets beat the Cardinals 8–2.

In October 2011, Beltran watched on television from his home in Puerto Rico as the Cardinals, just as they had done in 2006, won the World Series. Beltran knew he would soon be a free agent, as would Albert Pujols, the Cardinals' star first baseman. As he thought about his future, Beltran knew that if Pujols left the Cardinals, St. Louis might be a possible destination for him. In December, that was exactly what happened, and Beltran signed a two-year contract with the Cardinals.

Wainwright, who had missed the entire 2011 season, including the World Series, because of his elbow surgery, was excited. He obtained Beltran's phone number from a team official and called to welcome him to the Cardinals. Wainwright left a voice mail message, and a few hours later, Beltran returned the call. The two chatted for a few minutes before Wainwright had the courage to bring up that at-bat five years earlier. If they were going to be teammates, Wainwright knew, there had better not be any ill feelings between two of the team's veteran leaders.

Beltran told him not to worry about it. "I don't even talk about it anymore," he said.

What Beltran was more focused on was getting to where Wainwright had been, enjoying that final October celebration.

"You play baseball all of these seasons to accomplish that," Beltran said after joining the Cardinals in spring training. "I've won a Silver Slugger, a Gold Glove, been to All-Star games. But I believe nothing compares to winning a World Series. At the point where I am in my career, I just want the opportunity to win a championship."

Beltran enjoyed an outstanding 2012 for the Cardinals, on and off the field, and on the next-to-last day of the season, he earned his chance to play in another postseason when a Dodgers loss to the Giants put the Cardinals in the playoffs as the second wild-card team. For the first time ever, a one-game playoff between the two wild-card teams on October 5 would decide which team advanced to the Division Series.

The Cardinals flew to Atlanta to play the Braves, who had finished the year with six more wins than the Cardinals. During that game Beltran had a hit and scored a run as the Cardinals won 6–3, moving them into the Division Series against the Nationals and putting him one step closer to his ultimate dream.

Beltran's dream of playing baseball for a living was born three decades earlier in Puerto Rico, when as a young boy, Beltran fell in love with the game that has now provided him with more rewards than he ever could have imagined. For that, he thanks God every day.

"I believed in God when I was young and went to church, but I never took the step of accepting Christ," Beltran said.

That happened in 2001, when Beltran was in his second year with the Kansas City Royals. Luis Alicea, a former Cardinal and a friend from Puerto Rico, joined the Royals that year and helped bring Beltran to that decision.

"He had a pastor there who also was from Puerto Rico and we went to his house for Bible study, and I just felt it was the right decision for me to make, to accept Christ and let Him come into my heart," Beltran said.

"Nobody forced me to do it; it was just the right decision for me to make. I had always been quiet and humble, and it made me understand a little more about how things work in life. It made me a wiser person, understanding things are under control, under God. We all can do the effort and put in the work, but at the end of the day, it's His will.

"When you understand that, you will do whatever you do and do it with the understanding that He is in control at the end of the day."

Beltran was a shortstop as a youngster, until one day when his youth team's center fielder missed a game and the manager asked for volunteers to play center. Beltran, fifteen at the time, quickly thrust his hand in the air. He enjoyed it so much that when the regular center fielder returned, Beltran stayed and forced the other youngster to find a new position.

A scout in Puerto Rico, Johnny Ramos, recommended Beltran to the Kansas City Royals. Beltran also worked out for the Expos and the Red Sox but was slowed at those workouts by a hamstring injury. However, the Royals selected Beltran, then eighteen, in the second round of the 1995 amateur draft.

Looking back now on those days, Beltran cannot believe all the hurdles and obstacles he had to overcome just in order to reach the major leagues. The first was communication. Beltran, despite having gone to high school, had spoken only Spanish all his life and did not know even a single word in English. The language barrier was a constant struggle, even when it came to feeding himself. Beltran, who was six foot one and weighed only 155 pounds when he joined the Royals' Gulf Coast League team in Florida, survived on a diet that consisted almost entirely of fast-food meals because he could point to a picture or simply order by number to get his food. When he occasionally went out with a teammate, he let him order first, and then said he would have the same meal—even if he had no idea what he had just ordered. He also battled homesickness. He was away from home for the first time and admits that he cried every night during his first baseball season.

Strictly a right-handed hitter at that point in his career, Beltran went back to Puerto Rico after the 1995 season and decided to become a switch-hitter, figuring that it would increase his chances of remaining in the lineup every day. He sought advice from a fellow native of Puerto Rico, the Yankees' Bernie Williams, and worked hard at hitting left-handed all winter. The next summer, Beltran was playing in Spokane, Washington, for the Royals' rookie league team when he told his manager that he was now a switch-hitter. The next day he went out and got three hits batting left-handed.

It also was in Spokane where Beltran began to educate himself in English, tired of not being able to communicate with his teammates and coaches, tired of not understanding what others were saying. One of his teammates, Rick Pitts, agreed to help teach Beltran English in exchange for Beltran helping teach him Spanish. The two worked at it every day, each learning a few new words.

"We went back and forth like that the whole season," Beltran said. "I was able to pick up a little bit. You have to be able to communicate. I was good talking to him, but talking in groups was a little difficult for me.

"It really took time for me to understand. A lot of people thought I was too quiet and that I didn't want to talk, but it wasn't that at all. It was because I was afraid and thought people were going to laugh at me if I said a word the wrong way."

That gradually changed, and even though Pitts never made it past Class A ball in the Kansas City organization, he played a major role in helping with Beltran's adjustment to living in the United States and understanding and speaking English.

At the same time, Beltran was learning how to be a better player as well. He had doubts about his ability when he hit only .229 for Class A Wilmington in 1997, but those doubts did not last long. Less than a year later, Beltran found himself in Kansas City, playing in the major leagues. He made his major league debut on September 14, 1998, against Oakland, getting an infield single in his first at-bat.

Getting to the major leagues, especially in such a short time, was a great accomplishment for Beltran, but he knew it really was only the beginning of reaching the goals he had set for himself.

He was determined to become not only the best player he could be but also the best person and teammate he could be, knowing it was what God expected of him in exchange for the ability He had blessed him with at birth.

"God opens doors for the ones who seek Him," Beltran said. "You become a better person when you sacrifice yourself and work hard and do things the right way. As the Bible says, God will put you in places you have never been before and have never experienced. I give all the power and glory and honor to Him for everything I have done in this game.

"I don't know what would have happened in my career if I did not have Christ in my life. I know I would have put in the work and the effort into getting better, but at the end of the day, it's His will."

Beltran said he became a better person, as well as a better player, when he fully understood God's power and realized that He was in control of every situation.

"We're all human beings," he said. "There are days when we doubt a little bit, but that's when a good friend comes along and lets you know about God's promises. It makes you understand that He's in control even though you don't understand what you are going through. At the end of the day, everything will work out for the good for those who believe in God.

"In my case, I know all of my experiences made me become smarter. I know how to deal with situations. When you go through a bad moment in your career you learn from that. Some people will say it's crazy, but you have to thank God for whatever happens in your life. I thank Him for everything."

Beltran's career has not included very many bad moments. He became the American League Rookie of the Year in 1999, at the age of twenty-two. He began getting MVP votes as early as 2003, and by 2004 he was an All-Star. That season presented the first serious challenge for Beltran, who was then eligible to be a free agent and had become a skilled and accomplished-enough player that he had priced himself out of Kansas City.

However, Beltran was comfortable with the Royals, and in Kansas City he was able to maintain a private life away from baseball. He had married the sister of one of his best friends from high school, and he and wife, Jessica, enjoyed the Kansas City lifestyle. He was worried that if he was traded, it might be to a place where he would lose some of his anonymity.

"I pray to God I can be a great player, but I want to keep my life," Beltran said that year, shortly before the Royals traded him to the Houston Astros. "I don't want to be hiding from people. It would be difficult to be recognized everywhere, so I couldn't do things ordinary people can do. I love to go to the grocery store or the movies or go to the mall and be an ordinary person. In Kansas City they don't know who I am. Same thing when I'm home in Puerto Rico. I like that."

Beltran's situation is not too different from other famous athletes and entertainers, who often experience the loss of their private lives as they gain celebrity. It was a battle Beltran fought hard, because he didn't think what he did—playing baseball for a living—made him more important than anyone else.

He did become more famous in Houston, as he had more success with the Astros and helped them reach the postseason during his brief stay there in 2004. He thrived on the national stage, hitting eight homers in the postseason, including four in their seven-game loss to the Cardinals in the National League Championship Series.

That performance helped convince the New York Mets to sign him as a free agent, representing a major test for Beltran's desire to remain a private person while playing baseball in the largest city in the United States. It was a challenge he thought he was ready to meet, thanks in good measure to his strong faith in God. He knew God would not put him in a position he could not handle, and he trusted God to take care of him during the rough moments he knew would certainly come his way.

It was a tough first season in New York, as Beltran's average, home runs, and RBI all dropped from the previous year. The Mets finished third in the National League East, and Beltran admitted part of his problem was that he did not have a good support system around him.

"I felt alone," he said after that season. "I didn't have that person, when I was having difficult moments, that I could feel confident and comfortable to go to them."

It was a case, Beltran realized later, when he should have confided more in God.

"Baseball is a tough sport," he said. "You have to understand that not every day is going to be a good day. In my case, the difference was between understanding that God has control and understanding you have the power. I understand He has control, and I go out there and approach the game with the mentality of having a good day, but you realize, at the end of the day, that things happen for a reason.

"I'm not proud if I have a bad day, but I go home and say, 'You know what, God? I gave everything I had and it didn't work out for me, and hopefully tomorrow that will change.' You have that mentality when you realize He has that power.

"When you think you have the power, you don't search for help because you think you can do it yourself. When you accept Christ, and you understand that He has the power, you don't feel like you are afraid to ask for help. All you are trying to do is get somebody else's opinion and ask people with the same kind of beliefs you have. Those are people God puts in your way to help you out sometimes, and you can find the answers you are seeking."

Such a person came into Beltran's life in the 2006 season with the Mets, when another native of Puerto Rico, Carlos Delgado, was traded to the Mets from the Florida Marlins. Beltran now had that person he could trust and talk to, and the results showed on the field as he set career highs in homers and RBI and led the Mets to ninety-seven wins and first place in the National League East. He finished fourth in the MVP voting.

That year, of course, ended with the final at-bat against Wainwright, just another example of the up-and-down career that Beltran experienced during his six and a half years with the Mets, before he was traded to the Giants in July 2011.

"There were situations that got out of hand," Beltran told the St. Louis Post-Dispatch in spring training 2012, after signing with the Cardinals. "I felt the way they managed their situation was sometimes a mess for me. My time with the Mets, I have no regrets, though. There are no regrets. I feel in the years I was healthy, I did the best I could."

During his struggles in New York, Beltran had to keep reminding himself that God had a plan for him, and one day he would learn what it was.

"You have times when your faith is tested," he said. "That's when you have to go back to the basics in the game and in your life. You have to think about it, reflect on the moment, and trust yourself. At the end of the day, God will give you the answer, not on your time, but on His time."

The way Beltran played in 2011 in his time with the Mets and Giants, when he played 142 games, hit 22 homers, and drove in 84 runs, convinced the Cardinals to sign him to a two-year contract. One thing he knew about the Cardinals was that he would have that support system he felt he often lacked with the Mets, both because of his own stronger faith and the fact there were many strong Christians around him on the team.

"I knew about this team," said Beltran, who had played with Lance Berkman when he was with the Astros. "When we came here as the visiting team on Sunday, we always had chapel and they always talked about the big group of guys they had here. There are a lot of good people here, wishing you good. There are so many good Christian people here that it impacts you in a positive way."

Having an impact within baseball is important to Beltran, but so, too, is improving the lives of others, especially the young people in his native Puerto Rico. It is one of the driving reasons behind the project he first dreamed about years ago—building a high school where young, talented baseball players can go to get a good education as well as good baseball instruction. It is the same reason, as he has gotten older, that he has always tried to provide a helping hand to any young player who asked for his advice.

"I always feel that if you play this game for a long time and you didn't share anything with anybody, then I don't think you did good in baseball," Beltran said. "You have to pass on the things that make you successful and share that with other people. You want all people to experience good moments with you, and your friends, and at the end of the day the satisfaction after I retire from baseball will come ten to fifteen years from now when somebody will come up to me and say, 'Carlos, thank you for the advice you gave me.' That will be something that will be neat. That's why I am willing to share."

That philosophy applies to Beltran's faith as well.

"I've had some guys come up to me and say, 'I want to act the way you act. You're calm, you're relaxed, how do I get that?'" Beltran said. "I tell them what I believe, and how I believe in God. I believe God can change you to be the person He wants you to be. Sometimes changes can take time, or He can do it in the blink of an eye. For most people, it takes time. I have seen the changes after they made the decision."

Beltran's ultimate form of sharing can be found at the Carlos Beltran Baseball Academy in Florida, Puerto Rico, not far from where Beltran grew up. The school is built on eighteen acres on a university-like campus that houses both school and athletic facilities, including two major league standard baseball fields. The academy was Beltran's idea, and he donated millions of his own money to help construct the facility and led the fund-raising efforts to cover the rest of the costs. The school opened its doors to its first group of about one hundred students in August 2011.

The facility bears not just Beltran's name but his heart and soul as well. Every day during the off-season he is at the school, working and offering help wherever it is needed.

"Guys like me never had anything like it, a place we could go and get an education at the same time," he said. "We provide kids with a lot of information about baseball, but also about life. I talk to them about nutrition and about everything I have learned in my career. I try to pass it on to those kids. When you are young, that's what you need—information—so you can make good decisions later on."

The school is fully bilingual, with the students being taught in English as well as Spanish in the classroom and on the field. Beltran does not want any of his students going through a similar experience that he did as an eighteen-year-old rookie, not understanding any English and having to follow the lead of other players and do the same thing they were doing, nodding as if he understood his coaches when he had no idea what they were asking him to do.

Students have to apply for admission and go through a tryout process, with Beltran participating as often as he can. They have to have baseball ability, and also must maintain a 2.5 grade point average to be admitted and then stay in the school. Beltran has helped make scholarships available for students who can't afford to pay the yearly tuition.

"These kids understand that this is their opportunity, and it doesn't come to everyone," he said. "They have been blessed, and they have the chance to take advantage of it. Some parents have come to me and really thanked me for what I am doing. It is a great feeling.

"God has blessed me and given me an opportunity to make a living out of the game of baseball, and I felt it was the right thing for me to give back to try to bless others. Now kids have a place where they can study and play baseball."

The students also are taught about God, and daily prayer is a part of the proceedings.

"We pray before classes and before practice," Beltran said. "We select a different kid each day to lead us in prayer. We try to let [them] know the importance of playing the game the right way, but that it's even more important to seek God and have Him as a part of your life. He's the one who is going to give us the wisdom to understand why everything happens in our lives."

The school will graduate its first class in the spring of 2013. No doubt, the event will bring tears to Beltran's eyes. He already cried when the school held its groundbreaking ceremony and on the day the school officially welcomed its first students.

The tears illustrate just how important the success of this school is to Beltran. The only other time he admits to having cried in his life—other than during that first year in rookie ball—was when his first child, daughter Ivana, was born four years ago after he and his wife, Jessica, had gone through two miscarriages. His wife and the school are two of the loves of Beltran's life, but so is playing baseball, especially when it comes to playing meaningful games late in the season and then in the playoffs.

His 2012 season included personal career milestones—becoming the first switch-hitter in history to hit 300 homers and steal 300 bases, and recording the 2,000th hit of his career.

He also topped the thirty-homer mark for the fourth time in his career, making him only the sixth player in franchise history to hit thirty or more home runs in his first season in St. Louis.

On September 30, 2012, as the Cardinals closed in on a postseason berth, Beltran hit his final two homers of the regular season, one from each side of the plate. It was the ninth time he had done that, and the thirty-fourth multi-homer game of his career. What it meant most to Beltran, however, was that it helped bring the Cardinals to the edge of clinching a spot in the postseason. That became official two days later.

"It's always good to have a good day, but this is not about one day," Beltran said. "It's about being able to go out there and win ballgames, and it's not about me, it's about the team. We have an opportunity to be in the postseason."

As Beltran's life and career have proved, given that chance, he intends to make the most of it. It's why his favorite Bible verse is Philippians 4:13. That verse, Beltran says, sums up his life.

"To me, it's real," he said. "Every day we live it. I apply it to my life every day. Every time I take the field, I tell Him, 'I'm doing this in Your name.' When I want to accomplish things, I feel like I can. But it's not for myself, but for Him and His glory."

SEVENTEEN

THE POSTSEASON

Consider it pure joy, my brothers and sisters, whenever you face trials
of many kinds, because you know that the testing of your faith produces
perseverance. Let perseverance finish its work so that you may be
mature and complete, not lacking anything.

—James 1:2–4 NIV

The congregation of First Baptist Church in Dalton, Georgia,
was faced with a conflict of allegiances when the Cardinals and
Braves were paired in the first-ever wild-card play-in game to
begin baseball's 2012 postseason.

Dalton, located one hundred miles north of Atlanta, is home
mostly to Braves fans, as could be expected. Many of the town's
residents, and especially the members of the First Baptist Church
family, however, also are big fans of Cardinals' reliever Mitchell
Boggs.

Boggs is one of them, having grown up in Dalton, and is a
regular at the church services when he is home in the off-season.
The best way to look at the game, church leaders said, was that it
really was a win-win situation—either Boggs and the Cardinals,
or the Braves, would win and advance to the Division Series.

The Cardinals, who had taken advantage of the Braves' collapse in 2011 to even make it into the playoffs, took advantage of the additional wild-card entry to make it in 2012, having finished six games behind the Braves in the regular season. The new win-or-go-home format really wasn't new for them, however, as they had played and won four times in the 2011 postseason when a loss would have ended their season.

In a one-game series, however, the Cardinals knew one mistake or one great play could make the difference in either winning the game and advancing, or losing and going home. In the end, this game was decided by three errors by the Braves and a controversial call by an umpire. The Cardinals took advantage, winning 6–3.

The controversial call came from left-field umpire Sam Holbrook, who called an infield fly on a pop fly by the Braves' Andrelton Simmons in the eighth inning, with two runners on base and one out. The call was made despite the fact that the pop-up was actually in left field. Cardinals' shortstop Pete Kozma had gone back and appeared in position to make the catch, but at the last minute he veered off, thinking left fielder Matt Holliday was there to catch it. Instead, the ball fell harmlessly to the ground.

If the play had not been called an infield fly, the Braves would have had the bases loaded and pinch-hitter Brian McCann coming to the plate to face Jason Motte, trailing 6–3. Instead, there were two outs and two runners on, and Motte was able to get out of the inning—but not before Atlanta fans created a nineteen-minute delay, showing their displeasure by littering the field with debris.

"You don't see something like that happen very often really, except for maybe an English soccer match," said the Cardinals' Lance Berkman. "Hopefully it will be memorable for other reasons, like maybe the start of another postseason run for us.

"That wasn't the story of the game in my opinion. It was the three errors they made that basically gave us about five runs. You can blame the umpires all you want, but in reality they didn't play good enough defense to win the game, and we took advantage of their mistakes."

Manager Mike Matheny was well aware that most people expected the Cardinals to lose the game, and that didn't bother him at all.

"I hope they keep not giving us any chances," Matheny said. "I think these guys have thrived on that in the past. I don't think they could have been more underdogs than they were last year and they learned from that. I think what that does is either distracts you or draws you together. . . . They believe in each other. We've got a good team. They are exciting to watch, and hopefully it will be more enjoyable the further we go."

Their opponent in the Division Series was the Washington Nationals, the champions of the National League East who brought a playoff team back to the nation's capital for the first time since 1933. The matchup featured the oldest manager in the majors, sixty-nine-year-old Davey Johnson, against the youngest, the forty-two-year-old Matheny.

Matheny was more concerned about the matchup of the two teams, even though Johnson had managed forty-seven postseason games in his career, compared to one for Matheny. As it turned out, the matchup that counted most in the series's opening game came in the eighth inning, when Matheny elected to bring left-handed reliever Marc Rzepczynski in to face pinch-hitter Tyler Moore with two runners on base and the Cardinals clinging to a 2–1 lead.

Moore won the battle, redirecting a 2–2 pitch into right field to score both runs and give the Nationals a 3–2 lead, which turned out to be the final score as Washington won the series opener.

The Cardinals could have made Matheny's decision easier had Allen Craig and Yadier Molina not swung at the first pitch in consecutive at-bats an inning earlier, both times with the bases loaded. Craig grounded into a force out at the plate and Molina hit into a double play.

"We had opportunities to win this and put more than the couple of runs we had up there," Matheny said. "We have been very good lately in situations, getting situational hitting done, and today it just didn't work."

The loss obscured a good start by Adam Wainwright, who became the first Cardinals pitcher to strike out ten or more batters in a postseason game since Bob Gibson in the 1968 World Series.

One skill the Cardinals showed during their 2011 postseason run, and which had continued through the 2012 regular season, was resiliency. One tough loss after another, the team was able to regroup and put together a good game the following day. They wasted no time doing that again in game two of the series, hitting four home runs, two by Carlos Beltran, en route to a 12–4 win, which sent the series to Washington even at one win apiece.

"The easy thing for everyone to do would be put our head down and get upset after a tough loss, but [that] doesn't get anyone anywhere," said Allen Craig, who had one of the other home runs. "We stay positive and worry about the present day and focus on the job we have to do, and then good things happen. That's what we're doing right now.

"That's kind of the way we've gone about it all season, taking it one day at a time. It's kind of a cliché, but it's really worked for our team. We forget what happened yesterday and worry about today."

While many of the Cardinals were relying on their experiences from the previous October, Beltran had to think back six years to the last time he was in the playoffs.

"I'm grateful," he said. "I just want to go out there and

contribute. Who doesn't love to play in these types of games, where you are fighting to win a championship? For me, I'm going to enjoy it because you never know when it will be the last time you are going to be in this situation."

Another player who was not with the Cardinals in 2011, but unlike Beltran, had never been in a playoff environment, came up big for the team as the series shifted to Washington. Rookie shortstop Pete Kozma hit a three-run homer to help lead St. Louis to an 8–0 win, opening a 2–1 lead in the best-of-five series. Kozma was recalled from Triple-A at the end of August after shortstop Rafael Furcal was injured, and the spark he had given the team in the final month of the regular season continued in this game.

"We had a huge void when we lost Furcal," Matheny said. "We put [Kozma] in there, gave him the opportunity, and he absolutely ran away with it. Just catching the ball out there was something we were looking forward to him doing, let alone having big hits, and then on top of that, being able to supply some power and run production.

"He's going about it the right way. I just want him to keep it going, nothing different. Keep the same approach. There are going to be more distractions; the better he does, the more times he comes through like he has, it will continue to be an opportunity for him to show resolve and mental toughness."

The Cardinals could have closed out the series in game four, but that would have been too easy for a team that had done nothing in that manner for two seasons. Jayson Werth's walk-off homer at the end of a thirteen-pitch battle against Lance Lynn in the bottom of the ninth inning gave the Nationals a 2–1 win, setting up the decisive fifth game.

With Adam Wainwright on the mound, the Cardinals felt confident, but it did not take long for that feeling to evaporate. The Nationals built a quick 6–0 lead, knocking Wainwright out of the game—and as far as most observers were concerned, knocking the Cardinals out of the playoffs. That was not the feeling in the St. Louis dugout, however. Even as Wainwright was walking off the mound, he was encouraging his teammates, "Pick me up boys, pick me up."

Chris Carpenter and Skip Schumaker served as the cheerleaders, pumping up the rest of the team, reminding them the game was far from over. As the Cardinals offense began to chip away at the lead, the enthusiasm increased.

"There was a life to that bench like I've never seen," Matheny would say after the game.

The comeback reached 6–5 before Washington got a run in the bottom of the eighth to make the lead 7–5 going into the ninth. Carlos Beltran doubled to lead off the inning, the fifth time he had reached base in the game, on three hits and two walks. Beltran became only the second player in postseason history to reach base five times via hits, walks, or hit by pitch in a win-or-go-home situation. The other player to do so was Babe Ruth.

With two outs and Beltran still on base, both Yadier Molina and David Freese, down to their last strike, worked walks. Daniel Descalso then came through with a two-run single to tie the game at 7, and Pete Kozma followed with another single that drove in two more runs, giving the Cardinals a 9–7 lead and touching off a major celebration.

When Motte closed out the game in the bottom of the ninth, the Cardinals had completed the greatest postseason comeback in an elimination game in baseball history. Only twice before had a team rallied from a four-run deficit to win an elimination game. Only once before had a team trailed by two runs going to the ninth inning of a winner-take-all game and won the game.

"It's just the kind of people they are," Matheny said. "They believe in themselves. They believe in each other. It's been this style of team all season long. They just don't quit, and I think that says a lot about their character."

Before the champagne was popped in the clubhouse, Wainwright asked for quiet so he could address his teammates.

"I told them all, 'I'm just real proud to be a St. Louis Cardinal, and to be your teammate right now,'" Wainwright would say later. "That show of heart, and that show of fortitude right there? It was special for me to watch. It was just special for the fans to watch. I was taken aback, and moved, by what they'd done. I just felt I needed to tell the guys just what it meant to me, and a lot of people who love the Cardinals. This is an amazing team. Don't ever doubt our hearts. Because we have heart."

The Cardinals' charter flight left Washington shortly after 3:00 a.m. on the cross-country trip to San Francisco, where the Giants were waiting in the National League Championship Series. They had completed their own unexpected comeback to advance, having rallied after losing the first two games of their series against Cincinnati, at home, to win three consecutive games on the road.

David Freese and Carlos Beltran got the series started on a positive note for the Cardinals with matching two-run homers, carrying the team to a 6–4 victory in the series opener. For Freese, it was the sixth postseason homer of his career, in only twenty-five games, and increased his career postseason RBI total to 25—the only player in history with more RBI in his first twenty-five postseason games was Lou Gehrig.

Beltran continued to put himself among elite company as well. His homer was the fourteenth of his career in the postseason, in twenty-nine games, and his career on-base plus slugging (OPS) in the postseason was the highest of any player in history.

"I'm really enjoying myself," Beltran said. "Good things are happening."

The Giants came back to win game two 7–1, and when Beltran had to come out of game three after his first-inning at-bat because of a sore knee, there was a reason for Cardinals fans to be concerned.

It turned out, however, that rookie Matt Carpenter, who replaced Beltran in right field, came up with the biggest hit of his career—a two-run homer off Matt Cain in the third inning—which sent the Cardinals to a 3–1 victory.

"It all happened so fast, which really sometimes can be a blessing because it doesn't give you any time to think," Carpenter said. "When a guy like Carlos goes down, it can kind of be a let-down for the team and I wanted to do something that would bring some life back. That at-bat was important for what was at stake, but also to bring life back to the dugout. I was glad I could get it done."

That was the same attitude Wainwright had when he went to the mound to start game four for the Cardinals, his first game since the almost-disastrous performance in the fifth game of the division series against Washington.

"A little part of me wanted to re-prove it to myself that I could go out there and pitch great when we need me to," Wainwright said. "I knew I could. I was very confident in my ability and my stuff. I just needed to trust it and go out there and make pitches."

That was exactly what he did, pitching the Cardinals to an 8–3 victory, allowing only one run on four hits through seven innings. The win gave St. Louis a three-to-one advantage in the series, one win away from a consecutive National League pennant and a return trip to the World Series.

Getting to this point had been Wainwright's goal all season, after he had been forced to sit and watch the 2011 run to the world championship because of his arm injury.

"In the off-season I was just like, 'Can we please do that again next year?'" Wainwright said. "As a competitor I just wanted to be out there so badly last year when we were going through that great run and I couldn't do a thing about it. As painful as it was not being able to help last year, I feel like I'm a major contributor this year and I'm having a lot of fun doing it."

One Cardinal who was not playing as well as he would have liked in the series was Matt Holliday, and it was revealed after the game that he had been dealing with more than baseball. Holliday acknowledged that his mother, Kathy, had undergone surgery earlier that day in a St. Louis-area hospital after being diagnosed with colon cancer.

"It's been hard," Holiday told the *St. Louis Post-Dispatch*. "This week's been hard. It's part of life, part of being a big boy. You've got to deal with what happens in your life. I wish it wasn't. But it's part of it. She's doing good and we've had great support."

The Cardinals hoped they could close out the Giants in the fifth game, winning the series at home and avoiding a trip back to San Francisco, but a couple of missed opportunities on offense and a throwing error by pitcher Lance Lynn sealed their fate in a 5–0 loss to Barry Zito.

Given that opening, the Giants responded with a 6–1 victory in game six, setting up the first seventh game in a National League Championship Series since the Cardinals beat the Mets in game seven in 2006—the series that ended when Wainwright froze Beltran with a called strike three. Maybe this game seven would be different for Beltran, allowing him to replace that memory with a much happier moment.

That would have created a great story, but it turned out that this night offered a reminder that dreams don't always come true, and dealing with disappointment and adversity will always be a fact of life, providing more moments when God is called upon for help and counsel.

The Cardinals were never in the game, losing 9–0, as the Giants moved on to their second World Series in three years. At least fate intervened and prevented Beltran from once again making the final out of a National League Championship Series, as he drew a walk with two outs in the ninth, before Holliday's pop out ended the game and the series.

Beltran's disappointment and sadness at coming so close to his dream of playing in the World Series was obvious in the clubhouse after the game. The fact that the Cardinals fell one game short certainly was not Beltran's fault. He hit .357 in the postseason with three home runs.

"There are a lot of players who don't make it to the World Series," Beltran told the *Post-Dispatch*. "Don't feel sorry for me. I was trying the best I could to get there and it just didn't happen."

Beltran will be back on the Cardinals in 2013, and he hopes to find himself in the same position again—needing one win to earn a spot in the World Series. He just hopes for a different outcome.

"Only God knows that," Beltran told the newspaper. "Next year is going to be another test. We should feel good about the team that we have. If we're good enough to get to this point this year, maybe next year we can do it again."

For those players who had experienced the joy of winning the World Series the previous year, to come within one game of getting the opportunity to get there again, only to lose, was a major disappointment. Like all such moments in life, it was a time for them to call on their faith, and to see a bigger picture.

"I think you are disappointed when you are in that situation whether you are a follower of Christ or not," said outfielder Matt Holliday. "Obviously, having a bigger perspective that's eternal helps you deal with worldly disappointments."

The end of the season is always a time for reflection, whether it was a good year or a bad year, and Holliday said it was important to remember all of the good things that had happened during the year instead of concentrating on the last couple of games.

"A lot of things go into a season like that," Holliday said. "Our ultimate goal was not accomplished, but you look back at the season and think about what we did accomplish. That's the perspective of baseball. We had a great season. We made a lot of bonds, a lot of relationships were developed. We just didn't win. The Giants were the team that won this year."

Third baseman David Freese, one of the heroes of the 2011 postseason run, also preferred to think about all of the good things that went the Cardinals' way in 2012 instead of reflecting on a couple of poor games.

"When you lose a game like that and the season ends that way, you sit down and reflect on all of the good things that happened during the year, especially the things that God has put in front of you, the relationships that He has brought about," Freese said. "That's what everyone needs to think about.

"We did so many good things, and you just appreciate all of the hard work that everyone put in, and all of the things God has allowed you to be a part of."

Before the clubhouse doors were opened and the media allowed to enter after the final game, Lance Berkman addressed his teammates for the final time, knowing he would not be a Cardinal in 2013 and would not have this forum again.

"They're going to be back," Berkman said in summarizing his message. "This Cardinals team is not going anywhere. I really feel good about the group of players the Cardinals organization has. We have a lot of young guys in here. I think they're set up well for the next several years."

Those players include Trevor Rosenthal, who became a national story in the postseason with his 100-mph fastball. In 8 2/3 innings in seven games in October, the twenty-two-year-old right-hander allowed only two hits and two walks while striking out fifteen. Young pitchers Joe Kelly and Shelby Miller also displayed a great deal of promise for the future, joining the veterans such as Wainwright, Motte, Boggs, and the rest of the pitching staff.

The regular lineup of Holliday, Freese, Beltran, Molina, Allen Craig, and Jon Jay also is set to return, and it soon will be bolstered by the arrival in St. Louis of youngsters such as Kolten Wong and Oscar Taveras.

Matheny, moments after the end to his rookie season as manager, was already focusing on the future, but he knows he will never forget what he had just experienced over the past nine months, beginning in February in Florida when the defending world champions went through their first spring training drills.

"Really what I've learned is that we've got a special group of players on our side who have overcome a lot of obstacles and did a lot of things people didn't think they could do," Matheny said. "There is quite a bit to be excited about if you are a St. Louis Cardinal[s] fan, and I want to make sure these guys don't forget how we got here, and the character and the heart that it took to be where we are right now. It wasn't how we scripted it to finish, but it was a still a great run that these guys need to be very proud of."

Matheny was talking about his team, but he just as easily could have been speaking about himself. He, too, had enjoyed a season he will never forget.

EIGHTEEN

MIKE MATHENY

For God did not send his Son into the world to condemn the world, but to save the world through him.

—John 3:17 NIV

Three days after the disappointing end to the Cardinals' season, Mike Matheny got together with reporters in his office at Busch Stadium to discuss the year and look ahead to 2013.

Before he even spoke, it was obvious how far Matheny had come in his first season as the team's manager. When he moved into the office after Tony La Russa's departure, the room was almost sterile. The walls were bare; the shelves on the bookcases were empty, equaling Matheny's managerial résumé.

Along the way, pictures of past Cardinals greats had been hung on the walls; books and photos of Matheny's family were added to the bookcase shelves.

A lover of books and particularly of quotes, two of Matheny's favorites had been stenciled onto the walls: "Good is the enemy of great," and "To thine own self be true."

Both were there to serve as Matheny's personal mantras and as daily reminders of his mission as the Cardinals' manager, a job he grew to embrace even more than he had expected would be the case nine months earlier, in the first days of spring training.

Certainly there had been challenges along the way, heartbreaking losses and thrilling victories. There had been moments of second-guessing decisions that didn't work as he had hoped, and moments of joy that came when his players succeeded. As a rookie manager, Matheny dealt with personnel challenges, questions about strategic moves made and unmade, and personal obstacles of learning how to cope with being a manager while also not ignoring his duties as a husband, father, and child of God.

The lessons he learned along the way had been recorded for posterity, on the notepads that Matheny carried with him everywhere. He did not want to forget anything about his first season as a manager.

As meticulous as Matheny was in his preparation as a player, he was even more so as a manager, which should have caught nobody by surprise. Matheny began keeping journals a few years ago, after he was given a copy of David McCullough's biography of John Adams and made note of how many letters and notes Adams wrote to his wife and children.

"I just thought what a great thing it would be to pass along to my kids," he said.

So Matheny began filling out a one-year devotional Bible for each of his five kids, making notations in the margins about things he wanted to tell and share with them. He had completed four of the journals before he was hired to manage the Cardinals, which will make the journal for his youngest son, Blaise, particularly interesting.

"Andy Van Slyke recommended the [McCullough] book to me several years ago and challenged me to read it," Matheny said. "I'm not a history buff, and I was kind of trying to figure out what the purpose was, because it is a big book. As I got into it, I really got the concept of journaling."

Matheny's 2012 journal reveals how he learned something from every game the Cardinals played—from opening night in April in Miami through game seven of the National League Championship Series in San Francisco near the end of October.

"I hope that never ends," he said in his end-of-the-year media session. "I constantly have my antenna up to see what I can do to help these guys. This job is multifaceted. There is the people side, which is different than the Xs and Os side. And then you have to try to balance the personal side. I've learned in all areas, but I have not mastered any of it. I keep trying to take in as much as I can."

Matheny added a few days later that the lessons he learned along the way proved challenging to his faith as well as to his baseball education. As Matheny worked to establish the trust of his players and build relationships with them, he was constantly aware that he was being asked, in spoken and unspoken ways, to lead a faith-based life in everything he did.

"Everything that happens to you every day is a test to your faith," Matheny said. "I didn't necessarily give a proclamation of faith to the guys, but they all knew where I came from. I didn't want to be a hypocrite in their eyes, telling them one thing and living my life differently, because you can't hide it during a major league season. You are together too much.

"I wanted to be consistent in how I handled myself on the baseball side, and I wanted them to see consistency on the personal side too. Part of my motivation as a manager is the same as it was as a player: that I don't want to be somebody's excuse not to find Christ. There's enough of them out there right now, people who have been misled by Christians. I didn't want there to be something in my life that would cause them not to find Christ."

As the season opened, Matheny made certain his players

knew that he was a man of God but that he was not going to force his faith on others.

"I also told them I was not going to be a coward and walk away from opportunities, when guys ask me a question," Matheny said. "They need to know where I stand and where I am coming from. Hopefully I am living a life that is true to God's Word. I've also got to be man enough to talk about what I believe to be true."

Matheny tried to prepare for this job by reading as much as he could about leadership, and by talking with others who had been successful leaders in all walks of life. He took notes, and tried to find ways he could apply them to his job of managing a major league baseball team.

"I have to write," he said. "I take a lot of notes. I learn by writing. I kept multiple journals during the season, and I've been doing that for years."

There were many nights during the season when the notes Matheny jotted down after a game were not favorable, but he still considered them a learning tool. The notes give him the ability to remember why he did something and what the factors were that went into the decision, and he tries to analyze why it had been unsuccessful.

"What were my instant thoughts?" Matheny said. "I go through the whole thought process: This is what I was thinking, and this is how it all went sour. What slipped through the cracks? That's what I wanted to have documented. I'm going to go through it all over the winter."

Not all of the notes, of course, were negative. There were just as many, if not more, nights when Matheny's decisions helped the Cardinals win a game. He wanted to take note of those circumstances as well, believing they also could be important in the future learning process.

"There were times throughout the season I would have been

an idiot not to look at it: 'I did this and it didn't work, what could I have done differently,'" Matheny said. "If you call it second-guessing, I guess that's what it's called, but to me that's the only way you learn is to look at your mistakes you made and make the adjustment or have a real good reason why you did what you did and support the fact you made the decision you did. I don't know any other way to learn.

"It just sort of came along as I went through the season. Sometimes it was only three or four sentences that just summarized the game and other times it was longer paragraphs. That was nothing I heard from anybody else, just something I pulled together."

Some of the differences between Matheny the player and the Matheny who moved across the hall to the manager's office were how much more personal the game became in the new job, how much harder he took defeats, and how he was not able to forget a loss nearly as quickly as he had been able to as a player.

"When I played, I could have second-guessed myself fifty to one hundred times a game if something didn't work out," Matheny said. "It's all about learning and trying to adjust. . . . I sit in [the manager's office] now, and I think about it a lot more. It's a drastically different world in here than over there, but I love it. I love the idea as I went into the job that I wanted to help put these guys into position where they can achieve excellence."

That goal applied not only to their performance on the field but in their lives off the field as well. All of it mattered to Matheny, who had played for managers during his career who he knew felt otherwise.

"I want guys to know they can come in here and shut the door and we can talk," Matheny said. "That has zero to do with base-ball. That's the good stuff. I love baseball, but the fact they would be willing to open up and talk about life—that's the good stuff and the rough stuff. I wanted to let people know that I cared about them.

"I wanted to make myself available to them. I didn't have a game plan to be their buddy; that's not what they need. If they think the only reason I care about them is because they can go out and hit thirty home runs or drive in one hundred runs, if they think that's the only way they are of value to me, then I've failed at this thing. I remember being that guy on certain clubs who felt I had value only as much as I was productive. That made a lasting impact on me, and it's not who I ever want to be. That's not how I would want someone to treat me."

Matheny already had a relationship with some of his players before the 2012 season began. He had been teammates with Chris Carpenter, Adam Wainwright, and Yadier Molina. He played against Matt Holliday and Carlos Beltran. As a roving catching instructor in the minor leagues for a couple of years, Matheny had come into contact with some of the younger players as they rose through the farm system.

Others, such as David Freese, he had met through charity work in the St. Louis area and through making occasional visits to the ballpark when invited for Bible studies or chapel services. That relationship base was important to him, but he knew he had to build on it to have the type of season he hoped to have as a first-year manager.

Former players who had been teammates with Matheny, or been involved with him off the field, had no doubts about how well he would do as a manager, but they were still a little surprised that the learning curve seemed to move so quickly.

"You are under the spotlight as a manager," said former pitcher Todd Worrell. "There have been a lot of guys who got that job with a lot more experience, and it has taken them multiple opportunities before they were successful."

Worrell believes Matheny was able to enjoy success immediately because of his preparation for the job, his God-given ability to motivate and lead people, and his confidence that he was doing what he was born to do. Matheny knew God had helped put him into this position at this time.

"I think Mike understands his relationship with the Lord," Worrell said. "We are all called by God with the talents we have been given. Everybody is responsible for honing those talents."

Part of Matheny's motivation was generated by his belief that it was God who directed his path toward being named manager of the Cardinals.

"I can't look at this whole situation and all of the things that have happened in my life the last couple of years and not believe that it is not a complete God thing," Matheny said. "It has shaped my faith in a different way."

Matheny refers to his being named manager as his "Red Sea" moment, where God made himself real to him.

"It really was like a modern-day parable, watching the whole thing unfold," he said. "It's my opportunity to show my faith, and not just put a badge on my shoulder and say, 'I did all of this on my own.' I know I can look in the mirror and just as clearly as I can see my face know this is all a God thing."

One person who could relate to what Matheny's life was like as a first-year manager was Clint Hurdle, the manager of the Pittsburgh Pirates, who had been there himself a decade earlier. Hurdle also views history as the best teacher, and because of his experience, he tried to pass along some advice to Matheny during the season about what he would have done differently if given another chance during that first season in 2002 in Colorado.

"He has to rely on the skill set that God has given him, because He has given him some incredible strengths," Hurdle said. "Don't think about what you don't have. The only thing he doesn't have is experience, and he is going to get that. As long as he uses his eyes and ears he will get all of that he needs.

"You want to make everybody happy, and that's one of the challenges. You can't please everybody. You have to prioritize who you need to please. I had to go through a personal transformation about that. My wife gives me five minutes when I get home to unload whatever baggage I might or might not have from that day. But at the end of the five minutes, I'm done, and now she tells me I am a husband and father. That has been a major blessing."

Matheny admits the challenge of dividing time between his professional and personal responsibilities was one of the hardest aspects of his new job. Having been able to make his own schedule for the past several years had left him free to attend his children's games, to be there for special moments, and to arrange his work assignments when it was convenient.

There was no such luxury in 2012, which caused a lot of personal heartache. He was with the Cardinals instead of watching son Tate's games as the senior center fielder at Westminster Christian Academy, when he led the school to a second consecutive state championship. Matheny often had his cell phone with him in the dugout before Cardinals games, getting text-message updates from the high school game.

On the night of May 21, Matheny was managing the Cardinals in a home game against the Padres in downtown St. Louis, while thirty miles or so west of Busch Stadium, Tate, the oldest Matheny child, was graduating from high school.

"Kids at the school asked me to come speak at the ceremony," Matheny said. "Tate took the heat off me. He said, 'Are you crazy? They've got a game.' They replied, 'Yeah, but he could take a day off.'"

That was not something Matheny was willing to do, even if it meant missing the graduation ceremony, because he thought he would feel guilty about taking the day off and not being able to help the Cardinals try to figure out a way to win a game.

"I probably did a better job sometimes than others being able to compartmentalize and have that balance," Matheny said. "It definitely had to be a conscious effort, no question, because this job can be so consuming. We had a great year as a family, and they truly enjoyed the season. We had some great conversations with the kids. I didn't feel there were any times that a barrier went up that caused friction in our family because of this position."

There were times during the season when Matheny's team needed him more than his family. The Cardinals had been without Chris Carpenter since spring training. Lance Berkman was injured. Center fielder Jon Jay slammed into the wall, hurt his shoulder, and missed two months. Other injuries were piling up, and trying to find a reliable reliever who could bridge those difficult innings between the starter and the closer was proving to be a difficult task.

Still, Matheny never wavered. He kept his poise; he didn't panic. Players say they honestly never heard Matheny utter a single curse word during the entire season, even on the two occasions when he was ejected from a game for arguing a call. Even getting mad enough to raise his voice was a rare occurrence for Matheny.

"He's extremely even-keeled," said David Freese. "As smooth as Carlos Beltran is as a player, that's how Mike Matheny is as a manager."

The players who already had established relationships with Matheny were not surprised. Others learned quickly that was what they could expect, even when the results on the field were not going well.

"We've got a good group of guys who all pull for each other," Matheny said shortly before the All-Star break. "We talk our way through it. It's the only way I know to go about it, to be completely honest and blunt. It's not always what [the players] want to hear. My concern is more about these guys understanding, and I want to make sure we are all on the same page; that we are all in the same boat. We've rowed about halfway. Everybody has responded really well to the challenges we've had."

Matheny could have included himself in that group, talking about the personal challenges he had endured to that point in the season.

"I don't know if I'm smart enough to understand stress," he said. "Mentally, I feel drained, but I love that. I love the challenge of trying to help out by staying on top of things, trying not to miss things. Without question, it wears on me now more than it did as a player. The losses are a lot harder to let go for whatever reason. I did a better job as a player of letting them go and getting ready for the next one."

Having to replay one decision, one different move, which could have made a difference between winning or losing a game was one aspect of the job that Matheny really did not anticipate.

"It shows that you care," he said. "I hate seeing these guys get so close and not being able to push over that one last hump. I keep my notes, and I go over them to see if there was something maybe we could have done. I feel I need to do that to myself. It's the best way for me to learn."

One of the lessons Matheny learned during the course of the season, as countless other managers have learned before him, is that he became a better manager when his players performed better. He also became a better manager when the team acquired Edward Mujica in a trade from the Marlins on July 31, allowing him to create order in the Cardinals' bullpen.

"It was huge," Matheny said. "We were struggling to find that guy until that one piece instantly changed. Going through some of my notes after games, you could see that we had a small lead and lost it in the middle innings. That was a pretty recurring theme. We knew we had a void there."

The addition of Mujica, even though it was not one of the flashier trades made by National League teams, allowed Matheny to set up the back end of his bullpen with Jason Motte, Mitchell Boggs, and Mujica working the ninth, eighth, and seventh innings. Their success erased many of those frustrating losses the team had experienced in the first half of the season, which instantly upgraded Matheny's success rate.

The Cardinals had slipped far enough behind the Cincinnati Reds that competing for the division championship was all but impossible near the end of the season, but the team stayed alive in the race for a wild-card spot, with the knowledge gained from 2011 that all they needed to have postseason success was a chance to play in that tournament.

That was another of the challenges Matheny had to face. He was not taking over a last-place club building for success years in the future, with a so-so fan base. He was the manager of the defending World Champions, a team with high expectations of success, a team that played before sold-out crowds who had become accustomed to seeing their favorite team in the playoffs.

As the quote on Matheny's office points out, he would not want it any other way. He doesn't want to be good; he doesn't want his team to be good. He seeks greatness. Back in spring training, he felt the same way.

"I believe in every aspect of my life that I am called to excellence," he said then. "I believe, through my faith, that I am called to high expectations as a husband, as a father. This job will be a test to my faith every day, but I believe if I stay consistent with everything I do in my life, I will be the best manager I can be if I am true to who I say I am. I want to just be consistent with how I serve these guys and be consistent with the effort I put in. I have accountability not only to these guys, but to myself."

If Matheny thought otherwise, he never would have allowed

himself to even be interviewed for the manager's job, much less have said yes when it was offered to him. As he drove from his west St. Louis County home to Busch Stadium for that job interview in early November 2011, Matheny felt the hand of God on him, directing his path.

Matheny knows God was there with him all through the trials and tribulations of that first season in the dugout, and that He isn't going anywhere.

"I don't think I've ever been part of a team that had so many gut-wrenching games, not just close ones, but crazy stuff," Matheny said. "It happened all season long. But I believe that builds character."

None of the disappointments during the season were as hard as coming within one game of making it to the World Series, with three chances to win that one last game, and losing all three.

"You could see the frustration on everybody's faces," said Matheny about the loss in game five, the best chance the Cardinals had of winning the series against the Giants. "We knew it was right there. But that's just the way this game works. It was not for a lack of trying that we didn't get it done."

When he played in the major leagues, Matheny used the music to "Dive" by Steven Curtis Chapman as his walk-up song when he came up to bat. The lyrics have been important in Matheny's life both as a manager and as a player, when he was trying to win a job on the Cardinals during spring training but found himself really struggling to succeed.

"I knew I was choking off my ability out of fear, a fear of not getting what I wanted, which was to play for this team," Matheny said. "I was so engrossed with losing the opportunity that I had lost focus of maximizing my ability. The song became really important at that time of my life.

"The line in the chorus, 'Whether I sink or whether I swim,

I'm diving in,' really was accurate. I'm going all out right here. I'm going to turn this over, because He knows the plans He has for me, and they are greater than the ones I have for myself. I need to relinquish control of this, just like other areas of our lives that we try to hold on to.

"That kind of became my creed for as long as I played the game, that I was not going to be done in by a fear of failure. I was going to experience the freedom that I have to live this out, knowing He would direct my steps along the way. I was going to control what I could control, which was my effort, and take advantage of the opportunity. I was not going to throw it away."

The lyrics to the song are just as important now to Matheny the manager as they were during his playing career. He made the plunge into the managerial waters in 2012, and as he reached the end of the year, he had no regrets about the decision.

"The freedom that I have in doing this job comes from my faith," he said. "I just know where this opportunity came from. I know I am going to go about this in a way of glorifying God and realize that this was put in front of me for a reason. I am not going to have a fear of failure in this job. What that does is keep me from compromising, holding on to something so tightly. I love what I do. I absolutely love it. I also know people realize it is not mine.

"I've been given the opportunity to be faithful with the job I have. I want to win—that's my job and that's my nature. I'm going to do everything I can to make it happen. I also want to impact these guys along the way where it's bigger than the game. I want to impact them as people, to have an impact on their lives."

When he was playing, Matheny routinely signed his autograph with the added "John 3:16" Bible verse. This year, he changed it to "John 3:17."

"I'm not a fan of following ritual, and I thought I was missing the mark a little to continue to write the same verse," Matheny said. "I changed it to challenge people to check it out. They are both very important verses to set you positionally with God. You've got to have the right relationship with Him before anything else can happen."

As far as life applications are concerned, however, Matheny knows Proverbs 3:5–6 speaks louder to him on a daily basis: "Trust in the LORD with all thine heart; and lean not unto thine own understanding. In all thy ways acknowledge him, and he shall direct thy paths" (KJV).

One of the images that will linger well past the 2012 season is of Matheny and his team losing 9–0 in the ninth inning of the seventh game of the National League Championship Series, when a driving rain began to fall on AT&T Park in San Francisco.

As he had done in the one-hundred-plus degree heat of the summer, Matheny stood stoically on the top step of the dugout, head held high, face and eyes unwavering, as he watched the final outs of the season. The year might have come to an end, but Matheny knew his managerial journey had only just begun.

ACKNOWLEDGMENTS

The author would like to thank and salute all of the members of the St. Louis Cardinals who agreed to share their stories of faith in this book. In addition, thanks go out to two men for their enthusiastic support of this project, David Schroeder and Tim Ellsworth, whose suggestions and contributions were greatly appreciated.

This book would not have been possible without the contributions of my agent, Rob Wilson of Wilson Media, and the staff at Thomas Nelson, led by Matt Baugher and Meaghan Porter. Their work is sincerely appreciated.

Thanks also, as always, to my wife, Sally, and sons B.J. and Mike. Having them in my life is the greatest blessing I have ever received.

ABOUT THE AUTHOR

ROB RAINS is the author of thirty-one books, mostly on baseball and many about the St. Louis Cardinals. His list of biographies or autobiographies of Cardinals includes books on Tony La Russa, Albert Pujols, Mark McGwire, Jack Buck, Red Schoendienst, and Ozzie Smith. He is a lifetime member of the Baseball Hall of Fame and a lifetime member of the Baseball Writers Association of America. He is also the cohost of a daily radio talk show in St. Louis and an adjunct professor at Webster University.